THE GRUMBLER'S GUIDE
TO GIVING THANKS

THE GRUMBLER'S GUIDE TO GIVING THANKS

RECLAIMING THE GIFTS OF A LOST SPIRITUAL DISCIPLINE

DUSTIN CROWE

MOODY PUBLISHERS

CHICAGO

Unless otherwise indicated, Scripture quotations are from the ESV® Bible (The Holy Bible, English Standard Version®), copyright© 2001 by Crossway, a publishing ministry of Good News Publishers. Used by permission. All rights reserved.

Scripture quotations marked CSB have been taken from the Christian Standard Bible®, Copyright © 2017 by Holman Bible Publishers. Used by permission. Christian Standard Bible® and CSB® are federally registered trademarks of Holman Bible Publishers.

Some content in chapter 1 was adapted from Dustin Crowe, "A Theology of Thanksgiving," November 27, 2019, https://indycrowe.com/2019/11/27/a-theology-of-thanksgiving/.

Edited by Connor Sterchi
Interior and cover design: Erik M. Peterson
Cover illustration of flock of birds copyright © 2019 by grop/Shutterstock (767358181).
Cover illustration of forest copyright © 2019 by grop/Shutterstock (560104585).
All rights reserved for the above illustrations.
Author photo credit: College Park Church

Library of Congress Cataloging-in-Publication Data

Names: Crowe, Dustin, author.
Title: The grumbler's guide to giving thanks : reclaiming the gifts of a
   lost spiritual discipline / Dustin Crowe.
Description: Chicago : Moody Publishers, 2020. | Summary: "The Grumbler's
   Guide to Giving Thanks examines the biblical foundations of gratitude
   and traces how it can reshape everyday Christian living. When we express
   gratitude in all things, we praise our Creator and get to know Him
   better. Learn how to practice thanksgiving in both simple and
   extraordinary ways"--Provided by publisher.
Identifiers: LCCN 2020017855 | ISBN 9780802419859 (paperback) | ISBN
   9780802498779 (ebook)
Subjects: LCSH: Gratitude--Religious aspects--Christianity. |
   Gratitude--Biblical teaching.
Classification: LCC BV4647.G8 C76 2020 | DDC 248.4--dc23
LC record available at https://lccn.loc.gov/2020017855

Originally delivered by fleets of horse-drawn wagons, the affordable paperbacks from D. L. Moody's publishing house resourced the church and served everyday people. Now, after more than 125 years of publishing and ministry, Moody Publishers' mission remains the same—even if our delivery systems have changed a bit. For more information on other books (and resources) created from a biblical perspective, go to www.moodypublishers .com or write to:

Moody Publishers
820 N. LaSalle Boulevard
Chicago, IL 60610

3 5 7 9 10 8 6 4 2

Printed in the United States of America

To Melissa

I thank God for the gift of you as my wife
and your partnership as we learn to give thanks together.

CONTENTS

FOREWORD

Be thankful for what you've got. It could be worse."

For most of my life, this has been my approach to gratitude. Worse still, for most of my life, I actually believed this was a legitimate form of gratitude.

Having grown up in a working-class community in Appalachia, I know what it means to forgo things that other people might consider necessities. As adults, my husband and I have known similar scarcity, cycling through periods of un- and underemployment, both in ministry and outside it. But through it all, I never considered myself an ungrateful or grumbling person. After all, I could confidently open my Bible and affirm Philippians 4:11: "I have learned to be content in whatever circumstances I find myself" (CSB).

Yes, if there was anything I knew how to do, it was how to make do with little. Even more, I found a kind of odd satisfaction in doing it. God could count on me. I was one of His compliant children, the kind who doesn't make demands and knows how to accept whatever He gives.

It would seem, however, that surrendering to the limits of your circumstances is not the same as surrendering to God. Resignation is not the same as gratitude, and choking desire does not lead to thanksgiving. Because as the years passed, I found my heart growing more anxious and more inclined toward pessimism. I found myself offering up gratitude as a "tax" (as Dustin describes it in this book) rather than a gift. And slowly, I found myself struggling to do even this.

As I look back now, I can see that the reason I found contentment increasingly difficult was because I'd been bypassing the work of true thanksgiving. Instead of naming and affirming the Giver, I'd been content to forgo gifts and count it as gratitude. And so, for me at least, the journey to true thanksgiving began as God opened my eyes to His goodness, when I learned to see the world through the lens of His abundance rather than my scarcity.

Because just a few verses prior to Philippians 4:11, Paul calls believers to a perspective on the world that sees and seeks the goodness of God. In verses 8 and 9, he calls us to search out all that is true, honorable, just, pure, lovely, and commendable. And when we do, when we look for the work of God in our lives, we can't help but find it, regardless of our circumstances. So that in learning to see the work of God in our lives, we can't help but be grateful. And even in our need, even in offering up our requests, we can't help but do so with thanksgiving (4:6).

But make no mistake, thanksgiving is a learned response. It does not come naturally, while grumbling does. That's why I'm happy to invite you to journey through this book, to find your way toward gratitude. Perhaps, like me, your struggle is rooted in scarcity; or maybe it's rooted in consumption and having too much. But regardless of what makes us stumble along the road toward thanksgiving, the path is the same.

In giving attention to God's goodness, in giving attention to all the ways He is present and at work in our lives, we can't help but thank Him.

Hannah Anderson
Author, *All That's Good: Recovering the Lost Art of Discernment*

GRATITUDE QUIZ

The short quiz below might help you test where you land on a spectrum from grateful to grumbling. As honest as you can be, circle either (A) or (B) for each question.

1. Do you more often (A) remember God's blessings in your life or (B) forget them?

2. When things don't go your way, do you typically respond (A) in gratitude or (B) by grumbling?

3. Do you see thanksgiving as (A) an essential spiritual rhythm for Christians or (B) something that's great to do when you remember it but unnecessary?

4. Would you say you tell God thanks (A) daily or (B) less than daily?

5. Is thanksgiving (A) a significant part of your prayer life or (B) a small part of it?

6. Would you describe yourself as more often (A) content or (B) discontent?

7. As you go throughout your day, do you usually (A) have eyes open to reasons for giving thanks around you or (B) not see many things to give thanks for?

8. Do you tend to rehearse (A) God's generosity and goodness or (B) what seems unfair?

9. Do you (A) often tell others reasons you're grateful or (B) rarely talk about why you're grateful?

10. When you see things others have that you don't, do you (A) rest in what God has given you or (B) struggle with jealousy?

11. If you were to list reasons for gratitude, would it be (A) a long list and easy to come up with things to give thanks for or (B) a short list and hard to think of many things?

12. Is practicing thanksgiving (A) a regular part of your life or (B) an irregular part of your life?

13. Do you (A) have a place or way of intentionally recording reasons for gratitude or (B) not have a place or way to intentionally record reasons for gratitude?

14. When circumstances are difficult, do you (A) still find things to be thankful for or (B) stop giving thanks altogether?

15. When you think about thanksgiving, do you (A) tell God thanks or (B) feel grateful but not actually tell God thanks?

Now tally up how many times you circled (A). The goal isn't to condemn you but to reveal how prone you are to thanksgiving, knowing all of us have room to grow.

If you circled (A) SEVEN OR FEWER TIMES, then grumbling likely feels more natural than gratitude for you. If that's you, don't be discouraged. This book provides practical help to begin taking small steps away from grumbling and toward giving thanks.

If you circled (A) MORE THAN SEVEN BUT LESS THAN FIFTEEN TIMES, then you likely practice giving thanks with some regularity, but you know your heart often strays toward ingratitude or grumbling. This book can help you grow further and deeper in gratitude.

If you circled (A) FIFTEEN TIMES, then you're either an expert who has mastered gratitude or you lack self-awareness. You might still want to read this book, if only "for a friend."

CONFESSIONS OF A RECOVERING PESSIMIST

I want to be honest up front. I'm not writing as an expert. At heart, I'm a grumbling, pessimistic, need to smile more, glass half-empty kind of guy. (My personality aligns closer to Eeyore than Tigger.) My mind gravitates toward problems—and coming up with solutions—not what's working. But through the joy of recognizing God at work and responding to Him, my little tastes of thanksgiving and its life-changing power leave me wanting another plate.

Since expertise didn't compel me to write this, let me share four motivations.

First, I know the glaring need in my life. That's not a humble-brag; it's the truth. I study and write as much to learn as I do to teach.

Second, because few books address giving thanks biblically, I want us to grasp how much God prioritizes it for His people. While writing this book, people often asked, "What are you writing about?" I answered with something about thanksgiving or giving thanks. More times than I would like, the person then asked if it was for the holiday of Thanksgiving. November is a great month to practice giving thanks intentionally. For three years I've tried to maximize the month to cultivate daily gratitude.* But the assumption that giving thanks isn't a year-round practice further convinced me of our need to reexamine thanksgiving. Maybe the biggest "aha moment" came from noticing how the Bible highlights thanksgiving as a key way we better know and love God.

My third reason is because as we give God thanks, we delight in what we discover about Him. Thanksgiving leads to knowing God more fully, which leads to trusting in God more, worshiping God more, and loving God more. It creates intimacy between the Giver and the recipient. I want to draw nearer to God. I want that for you too. And God wants that for us. Thanksgiving will help.

And fourth, it's not only a way we glorify God, but it's a means of growing. As our faith and joy in God increase through thanksgiving, it cuts off the food supply to sin from ingratitude and idolatry. It's not an afterthought of the Christian life or the cherry on top of our spiritual disciplines. It's not something we get to when we think of it or when all our spiritual ducks are in a row. Giving thanks is an essential, life-giving part of the Christian life. It changes us.

---

* See the appendix for a Gratitude Challenge for any time of the year. It provides a thirty-day reading plan focused on thanksgiving, and practical ways to daily cultivate a habit of giving thanks to God. This would be a great exercise to do alongside reading this book.

MY JOURNEY

My ongoing journey in gratitude involved three key learning experiences pushing me forward. Like many seasons of growth, this one began with reading good books.

These books encouraged me to practice thanksgiving, which took it from a concept to a life-changing spiritual rhythm.[1] It began with a monthly challenge (similar to the one in the appendix). Every day I read about thanksgiving in the Bible while recording what I was thankful for. I noticed how thanksgiving squeegeed murmuring, complaining, and criticizing off my heart like stains and smudges off my car window. This new vantage for seeing the world changed my perspective and my responses. My trust in God and overall joy increased. I experienced firsthand the blessing and benefits of giving thanks.

But after the challenge ended, if I ignored giving thanks, the same sinful patterns and crusty behaviors returned. I'd criticize and mutter frustrations under my ungrateful breath. Irritation sprouted up and joy fizzled out. It became clear I needed to give thanks not just for one month or occasionally, but I needed it to become an ongoing practice.

A third link in my path included a project in graduate school and corresponding class I taught at church. For one of my objectives, I compared the emphasis given to various spiritual disciplines in Christian books to their weight in the Bible. On my list for things emphasized in the Bible but disregarded in popular Christian literature, thanksgiving and confession rose to the top. Both were crucial habits from beginning to end of the Bible, in all seasons and circumstances, and yet both often get snubbed today.

This confirmed what my earlier reading and practice of thanksgiving led me to believe. In the Bible, thanksgiving plays a prominent and powerful role, but we've demoted it to a seasonal add-on.

Our minimal understanding and practice of thanksgiving takes a significant tool for growth out of our discipleship toolbox. For my sake and for others, I want to recover it for today. I'm not approaching the topic as someone who has arrived, but as a fellow sojourner wanting to better follow and know Jesus.

In the Bible, thanksgiving plays a prominent and powerful role, but we've demoted it to a seasonal add-on.

While grumbling is natural, gratitude is supernatural. We need God's help. Gratitude goes against the grain of our hearts. It takes work. Developing the reflex of thanksgiving takes time and effort. But stick with me; the payoff is worth it. God wants this for us. He not only teaches us about thanksgiving in the Word, but He helps us grow in it by His Spirit. We'll depend on both throughout this book.

We need change on the inside. Biblical habits shape our heart. As we give thanks, grumbling gives way to gratitude. God-centered worship replaces self-focused whining.

WHERE WE'RE HEADED

This book explores thanksgiving with the following road map. Chapters 1 through 3 provide a biblical foundation. Chapter 1 lays out four aspects of biblical thanksgiving. We identify reasons to give thanks, recognize God as the Giver, express thanksgiving to Him, and better know Him through it all. Gratitude might begin with gifts but it leads us to God.

Chapter 2 builds out a theology of thanksgiving. From thanksgiving offerings in the Old Testament to presenting ourselves to God in gratitude (Rom. 12:1–2), Scripture elevates and expands the role of thanksgiving from beginning to end. While the second chapter unpacks the meaning of thanksgiving, chapter 3 considers its power. It gives a sample of the many areas the Bible applies giving thanks. Thanksgiving is practical. God's people turn to it to combat many of the struggles and stresses we face in life.

Chapters 4 to 7 show us how to weave this into everyday life. Each chapter in this section builds on one of the four features of practicing thanksgiving laid out in chapter 1. Chapter 4 helps us spot reasons to give thanks. We'll never practice thanksgiving if we don't feel thankful. And we won't feel thankful unless we detect reasons to give thanks. Chapter 5 takes a tiny step from *what* we're thankful for to *who* we're thankful to. Biblical thanksgiving is God-centered. To better recognize God as the source behind what we're grateful for, we'll walk through five categories. Each looks around to notice God's work so we can look up in thanks.

While gratitude might be an internal disposition, we communicate thanksgiving through words, songs, and prayers. Chapter 6 reminds us thanksgiving must be expressed. The last chapter of this section (chapter 7) ties things together by showing how this kind of thanksgiving leads to knowing and enjoying God. While giving thanks changes us in many ways, the greatest benefit is how it deepens our walk with God. We learn more about who He is through what He does and gives.

Chapters 8 and 9 teach us to give thanks in all seasons. Chapter 8 examines how the Bible links thanksgiving with remembering. Remembering in gratitude helps us rest in God as we look forward. We fight fear and anxiety not by looking in, but by looking back in our history and looking up in thanksgiving.

The final chapter tries to explain why the Bible calls us to give thanks "in all circumstances." We won't always feel thankful, and we won't always embrace with open arms everything God allows into our path. But biblical gratitude is gritty gratitude.

Even in trials, we give thanks, not for the frustrations or brokenness but because we trust God in them. He is still with us and working all things for our good and His glory. When we rest in God and believe His promises, even the most difficult scenarios can lead to thanksgiving. Gratitude is more about God than His gifts. We learn this lesson by giving thanks in both good times and hard times.

GRATITUDE IN A GRIPING WORLD

People are cranky today. Turn on the TV or scan social media and you'll encounter a choir of voices fighting, disputing, criticizing, and complaining. It seems like people look for something to be negative about. Cynicism and pessimism abound. Jealousy and entitlement tempt us daily. These sins have always existed, but it feels like they permeate life today.

The world is ripe for receiving an alternative message. Through biblical thanksgiving, the church has one to offer. The message isn't an over-the-top optimism. It's not about wearing a grin 24/7, having the brightest and whitest smile, or being positive Peggy (or Pete). Biblical gratitude is gritty gratitude. It's honest about brokenness and affirms difficulties and disagreements all around, and yet, it sees reasons to give thanks in all things. It doesn't sweep the junk of life under the carpet of ignorance, but it does find more reasons to be grateful than to grumble.

The church can show how the beauty and joy of gratitude offers something much greater than the ugly, life-sucking griping that's so common. But to have this voice, individual Christians and churches must regain the spiritual discipline of gratitude. We must learn how and why to give thanks on both the mountaintop and in the valley. Thanksgiving must shift from a once-a-year emphasis to a persistent practice.

In a fallen world and in sinful hearts, grumbling is common. I do it. You do it. I groan quicker than I give thanks. I ask God why more than I tell Him thanks. But I don't want to stay this way. I know growing in gratitude is a better alternative, for both me and those around me. I hope this book can be a guide helping grumblers become grateful.

CHAPTER 1

GRATITUDE'S BLUEPRINT

W hen people think of thanksgiving, they likely think of Pilgrims, not prayer; drumsticks, not doctrine. Even the holiday of Thanksgiving gets minimized and skipped over. Black Friday has taken over Thanksgiving Day for many people. The morning started with gratitude for what we have, but by evening, we're thinking about what we want next. In our day and age of more-more-more, where "Thanksgiving" is the waiting season between Halloween and Christmas, gratitude takes a back seat. It's no surprise it struggles to compete for attention with a holiday where I get to make a list of things people will buy me.

It's easy to blame the world, but I'll admit my guilt. I know God is the source of everything in my life. That doesn't mean thanksgiving makes it into my day-to-day rhythms like it should. I take gifts for granted and ignore His work on my behalf. When I don't get what I want, I complain and feel cheated. I'm quick to gripe and groan.

To fight our inclination toward grumbling, we need gratitude.

While we talk to God a lot about what we want, we also must give thanks to God for who He is and what He's done. We not only say "please" in our prayers but we also say "thank You."

As the psalmist says, "It is good to give thanks to the LORD" (Ps. 92:1). Not only is it right to give thanks, but it's *good* to do so. It's good because it glorifies God and bolsters our faith. It confesses everything we have ultimately comes from God (1 Cor. 4:7). It's good because it chooses joy over discontentment. We trust God in His wisdom and kindness for what He gives and allows (Phil. 4:4–13). And it's good because giving thanks opens a door to greater intimacy with God (Pss. 31:7; 100:4–5).

Are you interested in these things: more joy, less discontentment and envy, and a deeper walk with God? Keep reading to learn how gratitude opens a door welcoming them into our life.

While commending thanksgiving, I also want to caution us. Many books and articles equate thanksgiving with naming blessings. The focus becomes goodies rather than God. "I'm thankful for family. I'm thankful for church. I'm thankful for pumpkin pie and all its various spin-offs." I'm not the thanksgiving police here to slap anyone on the wrist, but I'd like to move from being thankful for stuff to also (and especially) being thankful to God. The object of our gratitude needs to expand from *something* to *someone*.

Acknowledging God's gifts is a great place to start. But we can't reduce giving thanks to identifying blessings. Biblical thanksgiving involves recognizing reasons to give thanks and then expressing gratitude to God for them. As we consider what He's done or who He is, we find joy in Him. In this opening chapter, I want to summarize these four features or steps of biblical thanksgiving. They will become the major focus of chapters 4 to 7.

1. Thankful
2. Thankful to God
3. Thankfulness to God expressed
4. Thankfulness to God leading to joy in God

I'm not suggesting you mechanically move from "step 1" to "step 2." They all go together. Over time, they'll happen at once more naturally. Like you might do with a toy or piece of equipment, we'll take thanksgiving apart and put its pieces on the table to understand how it works. Unlike when I assemble things at home, everything should fit back together without any unexplainable parts left over.

THANKFUL

Thanksgiving is more than a quick nod of the cap for the good stuff in our life. It's not a spiritual contract where God blesses us and we hold up our end of the deal by acknowledging Him. It should be motivated by grace and gratitude, not guilt or greed.

We often relate to God like we do with relatives at Christmas. Saying thank you is the right thing to do, so we do it. As a teenager, my grandma would buy me sweaters I could never wear in public. (It was almost as if she gave laughable white elephant gifts before that was even a thing.) They weren't close to what

I wanted, but she loved me. I knew the respectful thing to do was say thanks. And selfishly, I wanted to ensure I'd get a gift for my upcoming birthday (hopefully cash this time). I know, it's not very deep. But that's often how we view giving God thanks. We realize we need to do it more often, but our shallow grasp of what it's about keeps it from becoming a meaningful part of our Christian walk.

Thanksgiving should be motivated by grace and gratitude, not guilt or greed.

As chapter 4 explores, we lack gratitude because we're unaware of the mercies and gifts surrounding us. If we never take the first step of experiencing gratitude through seeing what we have to be thankful for, we'll never give thanks. We'll then lose out on joy and communion with God. Thanksgiving starts by not taking the gifts, provision, and blessings for granted. But feeling thankful leads us somewhere.

THANKFUL TO GOD

It's easy to stop at stuff I'm glad to have or people I appreciate, but there's a lot more to thanksgiving.*

If the first step is being thankful for *something*, in the second step we realize there's *someone* to thank. The Bible never speaks

---

* Another problem with this approach is it makes no room for giving thanks in all circumstances, including the things we don't have that we want or the hard things we've had to walk through that we didn't want. If thanksgiving is only about the goodies and great moments, then thankfulness is narrowly restricted to tangible blessings—as we define them. See more in chapter 9, "Gritty Gratitude: Giving Thanks in All Circumstances."

of thankfulness in general. It always points to a person. Corne-lius Plantinga writes, "It must be an odd feeling to be thankful to nobody in particular. Christians in public institutions often see this odd thing happening on Thanksgiving Day. Everyone in the institution seems to be thankful 'in general.' It's very strange. It's a little like being married in general."[1]

If on Christmas morning I'm grateful for an eagerly opened gift, I should be thankful to a person. Someone shelled out the cash to buy it. They sacrificed time in browsing online to find it or dared to enter the madhouse of a store during December. They worked to make money, which they could have used on themselves, and they spent it on me. I wouldn't have the gift apart from their thoughtful, personal, and sacrificial act. I'm thankful *for* something but I'm thankful *to* someone.

THANKFULNESS TO GOD EXPRESSED

Thanks isn't merely experienced; it's expressed. Tim Keller writes, "It's one thing to be grateful. It's another to give thanks. Gratitude is what you feel. Thanksgiving is what you do."[2] If we're thankful to someone, we thank them. We say thanks in various ways (spoken, sung, written, through an offering, lived out), but it needs to be communicated.

"Oh *give thanks to the* LORD, for he is good, for his steadfast love endures forever! *Let the redeemed of the* LORD *say so*, whom he has redeemed from trouble" (Ps. 107:1–2, emphasis added). Don't just feel it; say it. As we respond to God's goodness and grace by giving thanks, it pushes out resentment, envy, anger, and complaining. Thanksgiving power-washes away the sinful residues of ingratitude. In its place, the joy of rejoicing in God settles into our hearts.

Give thanks.

THANKFULNESS TO GOD
LEADING TO JOY IN GOD

Let's say you feel thankful, you recognize there's a person to thank, and you express thanks. If you're there, that's a great place to be and I don't want to suggest you're doing it wrong. What I want to propose is that there's even more to thanksgiving. Not the burden of more to do, but the joy of more to experience. Where thanksgiving really comes to life is this next part.

Don't miss this. I'm not just saying the giver is more important than the gift. I'm saying the gift tells me something about the giver. The more thoughtful or more personal the gift, the more meaningful it will be. And the more meaningful it is, the more I'll appreciate them because of it. It brings us a little closer together. It tells me about them and our relationship strengthens.

I think this final step is the secret sauce of biblical thanksgiving. It causes it to pop. It flavors and elevates thanksgiving in a powerful and personal way. When giving thanks leads to knowing God and, therefore, greater joy in God, it changes us. Thanksgiving is no longer only something we do but it does something to us. If we can get to a place where we realize thanksgiving points us to a person, it can then deepen our relationship with that person.

Returning to my Christmas illustration, the unwrapped gift reveals something about the person who gave it. If my wife gives me a gift card, I won't complain because gift cards can be useful. But as much as I appreciate a gift card, if my *wife* gives me one, it might suggest a lack of thoughtfulness or sacrificial love. But if she purchased a book on my wish list, or gave me a gift card to a specific restaurant I love, I would be more thankful because she picked something with me in mind.

In this scenario, I'm thankful for the gift itself, but the gift showed me specific things about my wife. It revealed her thoughtfulness, kindness, selflessness, and love for me in getting me something I desired, even though it required more time and energy from her. As I recognize this and thank her for it, receiving a gift and expressing thanks becomes a unifying relational act.

This proves true for thanksgiving to God. As we give thanks to God for gifts—which we can truly enjoy—we should also look *through* the gift to learn more about the one who gave it.[3] In doing so, we enjoy and love the Giver even more. John Piper writes, "We are able to see every gift as a beam from the sun of God's glory. Every joy in the beam runs up to the foundation of light and ends there. No created thing becomes a rival but only a revelation of God."[4]

Gratitude gives us pause to ask questions like: What does the nature of this gift tell me about the giver? What does it tell me about what they want for me or how they're seeking my good? How does what someone did for me provide insight into their heart, character, intentions, and attributes?

David Pao contends that thanksgiving isn't merely a polite

and proper moral act. "Thanksgiving in Paul is an act of worship. It is not focused primarily on the benefits received or the blessed condition of a person; instead, God is the centre of thanksgiving."[5] In the Bible, when people give thanks to God, they do so with one eye on the gift and the other eye on the Giver known through the gift.

As we take this step into thanksgiving, it builds our trust in God. Here our fears, anxiety, and worries get smaller as our view of God gets bigger. This doesn't happen because problems go away but because we've encountered a God who is in all circumstances still good, in control, at work, providing for us, and acting on our behalf. Giving thanks fans into flame our faith while pouring water on the coals of our fears and temptations. We rest in and lean on the God at the center of our praise.

Through giving thanks to God, we gain love for God, trust in God, and joy from God.

EXAMPLES OF THANKSGIVING IN THE BIBLE

This kind of God-centered, worship-filled thanksgiving pervades the Psalms (such as Psalms 9, 30, 100, 103, 136, 138, and 145). In Psalm 103, David begins by blessing God for specific actions on behalf of His people (1–5).

> Bless the LORD, O my soul,
>   and all that is within me,
>   bless his holy name!
> Bless the LORD, O my soul,
>   and forget not all his benefits,

who forgives all your iniquity,
> who heals all your diseases,
who redeems your life from the pit,
> who crowns you with steadfast love and mercy,
who satisfies you with good
> so that your youth is renewed like the eagle's.

As David continues, God's acts reveal His attributes and His heart. He doesn't move past thanksgiving but piles on reasons for gratitude.

The LORD works righteousness
> and justice for all who are oppressed.
He made known his ways to Moses,
> his acts to the people of Israel.
The LORD is merciful and gracious,
> slow to anger and abounding in steadfast love.
He will not always chide,
> nor will he keep his anger forever.
He does not deal with us according to our sins,
> nor repay us according to our iniquities.
For as high as the heavens are above the earth,
> so great is his steadfast love toward those who fear him;
as far as the east is from the west,
> so far does he remove our transgressions from us.
As a father shows compassion to his children,
> so the LORD shows compassion to those who fear him.
For he knows our frame;
> he remembers that we are dust. (103:6–14)

David thanks God for His actions but also for how those actions reveal a God who is righteous and just (v. 6), merciful and gracious (v. 8), unswerving in love (v. 8), compassionate (v. 10), and understanding of our weaknesses (v. 14).

We also find this in Paul's thanksgiving prayers (Col. 1:3; Eph. 1:16; 2 Thess. 2:13–14). He moves from giving thanks to the God-centered motivation behind it: "I thank my God in all my remembrance of you, always in every prayer of mine for you all making my prayer with joy, because of your partnership in the gospel from the first day until now. And I am sure of this, that he who began a good work in you will bring it to completion at the day of Jesus Christ" (Phil. 1:3–6). Paul blesses God for the work He's done in them, and rests in the God faithful to finish what He starts.

There's a deep theology of God under every statement of thanksgiving to God.

For our third example, consider the story of Jesus healing ten lepers in Luke 17:11–19. There's one man in particular who not only praises "God with a loud voice" (17:15), but he also falls "on his face at Jesus' feet, giving him thanks" (17:16). The grateful Samaritan sees Jesus as his Healer, Deliverer, and Savior. Thanksgiving responds to a person. The joy isn't only in what he received from Jesus, but also in what he discovered about Jesus. He finds more than healing; he finds Christ.

When we give thanks, we acknowledge something to be from the Lord and we adore Him through it. There's *acknowledgment* of a gift as well as being *affected* by it.

GROWING IN GRATITUDE

As you seek to grow in thanksgiving, recognize God as the source of anything you're grateful for, and reflect on what these gifts tell you about Him. Thanksgiving moves from realizing what God has done to revering Him as a God who does such things. It's good to give thanks to God for His provision. It's even better to see God's generous heart towards His children. It's good to give thanks to God for the spiritual blessing of adoption in Christ. But it's even better to delight in the God who clears our charges and embraces us in His loving arms.

Become more aware of God's work in and around you, and get to know Him through those works. Let thankfulness lead to a closer friendship, heartfelt worship, and heightened trust.

As you read this book, each chapter unpacks the Bible's teaching on thanksgiving and suggests ways to practice it. You'll hopefully be convinced about how significant giving thanks is for your everyday walk with Christ and your everyday struggles against temptation and sin. Practicing thanksgiving will push you nearer to the heart of God, the Giver of every good and perfect gift.

Knowing and loving God is the ultimate goal. If you read this and can list off blessings all day long, but they don't inch your heart closer to God, then it's incomplete. If your perspective changes and you can turn lemons into lemonade with the best of them, but you can't turn gifts into gratitude, then something hasn't clicked. Thanksgiving aims to get our eyes on God. To redirect our heart from grumbling to gratitude, we must know the Giver of every good gift.

Putting It into Practice

GRAB A PEN, PENCIL, OR HIGHLIGHTER

Mark the places in your Bible where you see thanksgiving, gratitude, praise, or anything connected to giving thanks to God. Underline, circle, or highlight things you see about God you can thank Him for. Read Scripture with eyes open to notice thanksgiving and reflect on what it teaches. Take the Gratitude Challenge (see the appendix) for a daily reading of thanksgiving passages and respond in gratitude.

START A JOURNAL

Whether it's with electronic notes, a journal, random pieces of paper, a Post-it note, ink on a sweaty hand, or any other way you can write things down, keep a "gratitude list." Record reasons to give thanks, including things you see in the Bible, attributes of God, blessings in your life, ways God is at work, His mercies, ways He's strengthening you or sustaining you in trials, or any other reasons you can give thanks.

CHAPTER 2

A THEOLOGY
OF THANKSGIVING

I'm starting to hike, camp, and find other outdoor adventures. Maybe I should say, I've daydreamed about and read into these things. I'm like many dads with my delusions of grand family trips. I envision leading them like Bear Grylls on wild adventures they'll remember forever. As I read magazines and thumb through books, I'm discovering a difference between myself, someone who occasionally hikes or camps, and true hikers and campers.

Legit hikers don't climb a couple times a year; they build their life around it. The financial investments alone to trek for multiple days with quality gear tells me it has to become a person's main hobby, not an add-on. Hikers plan their vacations and weekends around these trips. They might attend classes, strength train, or watch videos when they're not doing it.

There's more to learn about gear than I ever imagined. I presumed you just needed tennis shoes, a backpack for water and dried meat, a tent, and a regular old sleeping bag. I'm learning it goes way beyond this. There are shoes for every terrain and temperature. And why do I need a sleeping bag that's suitable for temperatures below zero? If it gets close that cold, I'm finding a hotel. If you want to go "glamping," even more choices exist: luxury tents, inflatable couches, portable pizza ovens, LED string lights, solar panels, espresso machines, and Swiss Army knives that catch, clean, and cook the fish for you. I'm not saying camping requires sleeping in the dirt or it should feel like a bad mission trip, but if your amenities are a step up from your own house, are you really camping?

My exploration into this backpacking world exposes how little I know, but it also highlights the differences between a person who hikes a couple times a year and a real hiker. In my world, it's still an aspiration and would be a bonus if I can work it in. It's not (yet) who I am. The same would be true for a musician, gardener, scholar, athlete, or artist. There's a gap between doing something sporadically and it being such a steady part of your life it characterizes you. But many things that start small evolve into a significant part of who we are.

Giving thanks needs to be cultivated. For most of us, it's not a consistent practice. It gets neglected and ignored. We must form the habit of thanksgiving to overcome our habits of grumbling, ingratitude, and taking gifts for granted. Recalibrating our rhythms requires commitment and patience to see it through. We'll start small and work our way up. We give thanks, and over time as our gratitude muscles get stronger, we become thankful people. The practice becomes a posture.

In this chapter, I'll survey thanksgiving in the Bible. This will set a foundation for more hands-on chapters to come. We'll first examine gratitude words to expand our definition of thanksgiving, and then we'll summarize how the Bible develops this rhythm. As the Old Testament progresses and finds its fulfillment in the New Testament, thanksgiving shifts from an infrequent, external sacrifice to the continual, personal offering of grateful living. As we get a handle on what biblical thanksgiving looks like, we can better put it into practice.

EXPANDING OUR DEFINITION OF THANKSGIVING

Thanksgiving includes God's works and gifts, but it goes beyond them. God deserves our thanks both for who He is *and* what He's done. We give thanks for God's actions on our behalf. We also thank God for who He is and for revealing Himself to us. God's glory invites us to lean in with wonder and exclaim the beauty of it back to Him. Telling God why we're wowed by Him is the worshipful response of thanksgiving. It's how we rejoice in God being God and us getting the blessing of glimpsing His glory.

It's like how the grandeur of nature causes us to take pictures and share them through social media, or even go old-school by printing them out. Think of what you feel in the moment when caught up in awe before creation and how you respond. Seeing the towering splendor of Mount Rainier as it rises high above the horizon, gawking up at the magnificent California redwoods stretching to heaven, or feeling the refreshing spray of Niagara Falls bellowing back up into your face—these moments do something in us. They awaken awe. They compel us to come back, tell others, post pictures, buy souvenirs, and cling to these memories. Other than what comes from such wonder, there's no immediate personal benefit.* You don't go home with a bigger bank account. Stresses at home or work don't vanish. And yet, these things fade out of mind when we are caught up in something amazing.

We lose ourselves in glory and want to tell others. That's a picture of what happens in worship. God's majesty evokes awe in us that must come out of us in praise and thanksgiving.

If we narrowly define thanksgiving, separating it from a worshipful response to God's attributes by limiting it to God's actions, we'll shrink its influence in our life. God's attributes are perceived through His actions, so the two are tethered together. But even when we consider God's nature above and beyond concrete blessings, we can thank God because we find joy and delight in what we see of Him. His glory kindles our gratitude.

> **God's majesty evokes awe in us that must come out of us in praise and thanksgiving.**

As God's people, we thank God when we learn about His attributes because who He is as God affects us. His goodness isn't an impersonal trait. It allows us to trust Him with our daily

---

* Though less clear or immediate, there are some tangible benefits from nature. Studies show there are more mental and physical benefits to nature than we realized. I believe this is rooted in enjoying and benefiting from God's creation and finding rest from our everyday idols and temptations. For more on this, do a quick online search of "benefits of nature," or read a book like *The Nature Fix* by Florence Williams, *Last Child in the Woods* or *The Nature Principle* by Richard Louv, or *Balanced and Barefoot* by Angela J. Hanscom.

stresses. His righteousness gives us confidence He will do nothing wrong, evil, or with unjust motives. All He is as God has a direct bearing on our life as God's creatures, but even more so, as God's sons and daughters. Because He's a God of grace, we become a people of praise.

THANKSGIVING WORDS IN THE BIBLE

The related word-group of *thank, thanks, give thanks, thanksgiving,* and *thankfulness* is repeated throughout Scripture. They appear around 168 times in an English Bible, including 106 times in the Old Testament and 62 times in the New Testament.

But like the sun tucked behind clouds, thanksgiving looms nearby even when we don't notice it. Thanksgiving is broader than the times we see "thanks" in the Bible. A family of thanksgiving words with different names all belong in the same house. It's aligned with other words in the Bible, such as *praise, bless, glory* (verb), *exalt, exult, confess, acknowledge,* and *rejoice.*[1] At times they carry slight variations, but they're clearly related and sometimes interchangeable. If we leave these words out of our study, we'll miss key puzzle pieces in our picture of thanksgiving.

Thanksgiving and Praise

Praise and thanks often show up in the same context or verse. Biblical authors link them as inseparable terms (see 1 Chron. 16:4; 29:13; Ezra 3:11; Neh. 12:31, 38, 40; Pss. 7:17; 30:4; 33:2; 69:30; 92:1; 95:2; 100:4; 107:22; 106:1).[2]

> I will *thank you* in the great congregation;
>> in the mighty throng I will *praise you*.
>> (Ps.35:18, emphasis added)

> Enter his gates with thanksgiving,
>> and his courts with praise!
>> Give thanks to him; bless his name!
>> (Ps. 100:4, emphasis added)

> And they sang responsively, *praising* and *giving thanks* to the
> LORD. (Ezra 3:11, emphasis added)

Paul gives further evidence of their overlap. He opts for using thanksgiving words because he sees giving thanks as including the notion of praise. Even in the context of singing (see Col. 3:16 or Eph. 5:19–20), Paul elects to use words of thanks.[3]

Praise and thanksgiving are both heartfelt responses to God in light of who He is and what He's done. They ripple out of us because they reside in us. Like my daughter's juice box overflows every time I put the straw in (can't they take out a tiny bit of juice?!), what's in us spills out of us.

Thanksgiving and Rejoicing

Rejoicing also closely relates to thanksgiving. To rejoice is to take joy in something, but it's a joy infused with gratitude.

My favorite drink is Dr Pepper. Dr Pepper is not the same as sugar, but let's be honest, you wouldn't have DP without it. Take out the sugar and you lose the drink (this is why all diet drinks taste so different from the regular version). The same is true of rejoicing and gratitude. They're not the same, but gratitude is a crucial ingredient of rejoicing. Take gratitude out of joy and you don't just have a lesser joy, you lose it completely.

Imagine a grumpy, murmuring person who lacks gratitude. We all have people like this in our life. My guess is you wouldn't describe that person as joyful. They're the rain on your sunny days. Now think of someone in your life you would describe as joyful. More than likely, thankfulness also characterizes them.

Gratitude and joy. Wherever one is present the other is nearby. In the following passages, notice the proximity and connection between them.[4]

> *Rejoice* in the Lord always; again I will say, *rejoice*. Let your reasonableness be known to everyone. The Lord is at hand; do not be anxious about anything, but in everything by prayer and supplication with *thanksgiving* let your requests be made known to God. (Phil. 4:4–6, emphasis added)

> *Rejoice always,* pray without ceasing, *give thanks in all circumstances*; for this is the will of God in Christ Jesus for you. (1 Thess. 5:16–18, emphasis added)

Gratitude produces joy, and joy is wrapped up in gratitude. Anything we give thanks for offers a chance to rejoice in God. Anything we rejoice in provides an opportunity to give thanks. By setting out to give thanks we also embark on a journey toward joy.

Not only do we see "thanksgiving" language throughout the Bible, but God talks about it with its synonyms (such as *praise*) and antonyms (such as *ingratitude*). It's tied up with the ways we worship and follow God. It includes our words, saying "thank you," but it goes beyond words to a heart full of gratitude, awe, and delight. Our study of thanksgiving must extend beyond a concordance or word study and include an ear listening for any tune that sings God's praise.

THE THANKSGIVING OFFERING

A study of thanksgiving not only investigates words but it examines practices and themes throughout the Bible. To do this, we need to review the "thanksgiving offering," the religious and theological context of giving thanks.

Leviticus 7:11–38 introduces the "peace offering," which includes the thanksgiving offering (7:11–16), vow offering, and wave offering. Peace offerings were unique. A person voluntarily presented a peace offering (Ps. 22:25). They weren't recurring sacrifices tied to any holiday, ceremony, or event. Unlike other offerings given to the priest, the worshiper ate the peace offering. It provided a meal bringing people together around the table, joined in thanksgiving to God. Sound familiar? The only thing missing is turkey and stuffing.

Out of the overflow of who God is and all they received from Him, Jews worshiped God through this offering. Those with a "willing heart" (2 Chron. 29:31) gave this sacrifice, not those compelled by ceremony. Genuine awe or appreciation prompt this kind of praise. God's glory provokes gratitude, and gratitude promotes God's glory (Ps. 50:23).

You see this in Psalm 107, a chapter recounting episodes from the drama of Israel's story. This history retells Israel's unfaithfulness and God's faithfulness. The psalmist looks to thanksgiving as the appropriate response, not only for former generations but for anyone who reads his words, including you (Ps. 107:1, 8, 15, 21–22, 31–32). "Let them thank the LORD for his steadfast love, for his wondrous works to the children of man! And let them offer sacrifices of thanksgiving, and tell of his deeds in songs of joy!" (vv. 21–22). The focus isn't on the object presented on the altar but gratitude within the worshiper.

God is not interested in our pious practices if our heart isn't in it. If our motives are self-centered, such as wanting to keep God off our back or on our side, then God says keep these sacrifices to yourself (Pss. 50:8–13; 40:6). But God loves authentic worship, whether it's in brokenness trusting Him (Ps. 51:16–17) or in blessing thanking Him (Ps. 50:14).

Do you give thanks to God like a tax or a gift?

If you consider how you typically give thanks to God, is it more like a gift or a tax? A gift is something you want to give God. Gifts can't comprehend everything you want to say to someone, but they're a small representation of appreciation. A tax is different. It's something you pay out of obligation. You might like its benefits, but you pay a tax to stay in good favor or avoid trouble.

Do you give thanks to God like a tax or a gift?

When presented to God as a gift, thanksgiving is the sacrifice God takes pleasure in. Do it out of delight, not duty. Give thanks to bless God, not to bribe Him.

NEW TESTAMENT OFFERING

The Old Testament thanksgiving offering reflected a person's willing acknowledgment of God's goodness. The sacrifice symbolized a greater truth: everything comes from God and belongs to God. The New Testament trades in the shadow of the animal sacrifice for the reality of grateful worship and devotion.

If you're familiar with the celebrity-chef Emeril Lagasse, his signature move is yelling "BAM!" as he drops in some spicy seasoning and kicks things up a notch. The New Testament does this by drawing from Israel's thanksgiving offering but ratcheting it up. We no longer sacrifice animals, grains, spices, oils, or flours; we present ourselves. BAM!

The discontinuity is clear in that living sacrifices replace life-taking sacrifices. Because Jesus fulfills the sacrificial system, God's people no longer offer animals or grains (Col. 2:16; Heb. 10:12–14). Now the sacrifice costs more and the act of worship is more comprehensive. We're called to not just make an offering but to be the offering. We don't give God something outside of us; we give Him ourselves.

Let's see what this looks like in three passages.

Romans 12:1–2

Though separated by eleven chapters, Romans 12 echoes language from the opening chapter (1:18–32) and contrasts two very different ways to live. Central to this comparison is the role of thanksgiving.

The first chapter characterizes the person far from God by their ingratitude, idolatry (false worship), and disobedience.

Romans 12 describes the godly by their gratitude, worship, and obedience (12:12). In his excellent book about Paul's theology of thanksgiving, David Pao writes, "If Romans describes the ingratitude (cf. 1:21) that characterizes those who refuse to worship him, Romans 12 calls us to offer all of ourselves 'as living sacrifices' (12:1) to him who deserves all praise and thanksgiving."[5] We either offer our life, day, and body to God or to false gods. Choosing gratitude or ingratitude plays a large role in which path we'll take.

Paul writes, "I appeal to you therefore, brothers, by the mercies of God, to present your bodies as a living sacrifice, holy and acceptable to God, which is your spiritual worship" (Rom. 12:1). Paul embeds thanksgiving in the language of a living sacrifice. Our act of worship shouldn't be a one-and-done offering but something we continually do.

Because *everything* we are and have is found in Christ, our *whole life* is lived with gratitude. It includes giving thanks, singing praise, generosity, prayers of gratitude, and retelling God's faithfulness, but these small practices build a larger posture of gratitude. The small choices and cultivating the right habits add up.

Colossians 3:15–17

Paul conveys a similar idea when he urges living a God-centered life. "So, whether you eat or drink, or whatever you do, do all to the glory of God" (1 Cor. 10:31). Colossians 3:15–17 says it a little differently:

> And be thankful. Let the word of Christ dwell in you richly, teaching and admonishing one another in all

> wisdom, singing psalms and hymns and spiritual songs,
> with thankfulness in your hearts to God. And whatever
> you do, in word or deed, do everything in the name of the
> Lord Jesus, giving thanks to God the Father through him.

Giving thanks to God (Col. 3:17) isn't an afterthought or an optional add-on. It's not separate from doing everything in the name of Jesus. We live all of life under Jesus' lordship *with* gratitude and *through* gratitude. Giving thanks articulates our worship.

Hebrews 13:15

While Jesus ended the sacrificial system through His substitutionary death, one sacrifice remains: the sacrifice of praise. "Through him then let us continually offer up a sacrifice of praise to God, that is, the fruit of lips that acknowledge his name. Do not neglect to do good and to share what you have, for such sacrifices are pleasing to God" (Heb. 13:15–16; see also 1 Peter 2:5, 9). We no longer merely give a sacrifice but we live as a sacrifice. Thankfulness for Christ's work swells up from within and surges out in verbal acts of giving thanks (13:15) and loving deeds to others (13:16). Gospel-generated gratitude pours into every nook and cranny of our life.

RETRACING OUR STEPS

Thanksgiving is an indispensable part of doing all things with joy, to the glory of God, and in the name of Christ. It's the essential ingredient to offering ourselves up as living sacrifices. It's the ministry we've been given as God's people and priests. And it's a key way we offer up thanks to the Son who offered Himself up for us.

Thanksgiving isn't a polite, courteous act we quickly say or write down, only to move on once we've done our duty. Giving thanks is the heartbeat of our worship and obedience. Walking with God leads to thanking God, and thanking God helps us walk even more closely to God.

When someone has been in a café or made bacon that morning, you know it because the potent scents of coffee and fatty meat stick in the fibers of their clothes. A teenage boy might spray himself down with an overpowering body spray. When you're around one of these people, you pick up on those smells, whether the enticing aroma of bacon (meat candy) or the unbearable smell of cheap cologne.

What aroma do you give off? Is it the refreshing aroma of gratitude or the stale stench of grumbling? The more we draw near to God's presence and give Him thanks, the more our lives will be marked by the pleasant fragrances of joy and gratitude.

When thanksgiving isn't something we sprinkle in at the end of a good day, our mindset shifts about the role it must play. It infiltrates everything. This must start somewhere, and a life of gratitude begins with little acts of thanksgiving. We choose to practice giving thanks for specific things as we seek to live gratefully in all things. (Chapter 4 will help us take a step forward by spotting reasons to give thanks.)

Putting It into Practice

....

LET THANKS SETTLE DOWN DEEP

As you practice giving thanks, let it soak in that this is a deeply worshipful act. To sacrifice an offering in the Old Testament was no small thing, and neither is this. When you thank God, you offer up a beautiful, valuable sacrifice God wholeheartedly accepts. Momentarily halt your busy life, stand before the Creator, and present to Him a sacred gift He delights in. As you say, sing, or write thanks, envision it going up to God similar to the smoke or scents of Israel's sacrifices. Let these thoughts seal in you the significance of what you're doing and lead to more joy in it.

OPEN YOUR DAY AS AN OFFERING

If we have the goal of both practicing thanksgiving and developing a posture of thanksgiving, we can start on the right path by presenting ourselves to God first thing in the morning. When you wake up, pause to pray and offer yourself to God as a living sacrifice. This could include giving thanks for specific things, acknowledging your whole life and this day come from

God and belong to God, or asking God to make you aware of His presence, provision, power, ongoing work, and blessings of the day. Start the day with an offering—the offering of yourself.

CHAPTER 3

THANKSGIVING: AN ANCHOR THROUGH THE STORM

We might know something is a good idea, but unless we're convinced it benefits us, we dismiss it. Results speak louder than theories. Most people know eating better promotes good health, but until they lose weight, gain energy, or overcome sickness, they don't stick with a new diet.

We don't make significant changes until we feel desperate or experience our need. My beach vacations quickly result in a bad sunburn. I'm pale with sensitive skin, which means I go from pasty-white to lobster-red after a couple hours of sunlight. After that first day, instead of basking in the sun, I end up hiding from it. Sometimes it takes getting burnt before I'm persuaded about the value of sunscreen. We are pragmatic, practical people. I pray because I know I should. But when prayer draws me near to God's heart and convinces me of its power, reluctance turns to eagerness. The same is true for thanksgiving.

In this chapter, I want to whet your appetite for how practical giving thanks is for your growth and joy. I'll survey ways the Bible talks about thanksgiving's powerful effects on us.

Think of this like how companies in cities take people on a bus or trolley tour. After packing people in like sardines, they drive past the major sites, covering a lot of terrain. These tours provide an overview, not in-depth commentary. That's my purpose in what follows. Grab a seat, buckle up, keep your arms inside the vehicle, and don't miss all the places the Bible spotlights thanksgiving.

Here's a sample of a few of the trials, temptations, or longings we wrestle with as humans and how giving thanks throws down a rope and offers a way out.

ANXIETY

For most of my life, anxiety and worry haven't topped my list of personal struggles. I wrestled with them occasionally, but it wasn't a daily battle. Having a daughter changed that (and many other things). I now regularly feel my chest tighten and mind race as I think she might be hurt, sick, or in trouble. In her first year, every fever and fall sent me into helicopter-parent mode as I faced fears about her safety, development, and health. I've learned worry doesn't call ahead or bother to knock. It shows up when it wants, barges in, and takes over.

We feel powerless when these forceful waves crash over us, leaving us staggering and frenetically trying to find our footing. Anxiety saps the life right out of us. As you read this, there's likely something that pops into your mind when you think about what causes you worry or fear. Some "what if" scenario lurks in the back of your mind.

Sometimes storms in life are personal struggles, but other times anxiety can increase because of local or global issues. The coronavirus pandemic sent shockwaves of fear and worry throughout our world. Though not everyone was affected the same, and people reacted in very different ways, it created a palpable angst in our society. Many people felt overpowering anxiety as concerns grew about sickness, death, the economy, unemployment or finances, and the loneliness that accompanied social distancing. Where do we turn when instability and uncertainty rock our world? How do we stand up and fight back rather than sit back and give in?

When we give thanks, we fight anxiety and fear by resting in God. Paul associates giving thanks to God with peace from God: "Do not be anxious about anything, but in everything by prayer and supplication with thanksgiving let your requests be made known to God. And the peace of God, which surpasses all understanding, will guard your hearts and your minds in Christ Jesus" (Phil. 4:6–7). Paul doesn't rejoice because God already granted peace, but he rejoices as the means to receive God's peace. Praise from the heart brings peace to the heart.

While we might be powerless to change our circumstances, one thing we can do is shift from clambering for control by trusting the one who is in control. We find peace not in fixing the problem or figuring out a solution, but by trusting God. Thanksgiving takes us by the chin and lifts our eyes up so we focus on God rather than the things around us. God is still good, in control, and with us. We can give thanks because His promises hold firm in bitter storms.

DISCONTENTMENT AND DISAPPOINTMENT

Whether it's discontentment with where God has you or disappointment over how things have turned out, these are not unique temptations to our day and age. But with the affluence around us and social media platforms displaying a highlight reel of everyone else's life, it throws more gas on the fire. How are they going on another vacation? Look how obedient and well-behaved their kids are. A quick scroll through social media can leave us stuck in the pit of discontentment. As life progresses and seasons change, we might feel the gap between where we thought we'd be and how life is in the ordinary humdrum of "adulting."

If discontentment has its list of disappointments we *feel*, create a separate list of what we believe to be true by *faith*. Thank God for the blessings we do have, for His good and wise plan, His timing in releasing His grace and gifts, and His faithfulness in every season. Rather than listening to our heart tell us what God has withheld, we talk back. We remind our forgetful self of all God's provision, care, blessings, promises, and mercies.

We will always have reasons to grumble, but we have even more reasons to be grateful. When in doubt, list them out.

Whether it's lust—rooted in discontentment—or jealousy, listen to Paul's encouragement to choose gratitude: "But sexual immorality and all impurity or covetousness must not even be named among you, as is proper among saints. Let there be no filthiness nor foolish talk nor crude joking, which are out of place, but instead let there be thanksgiving" (Eph. 5:3–4). A heart of praise chokes out room for sin to grow. By giving thanks, we choose contentment in God's good gifts to us and wise plan for us. When it's lacking, other things opposed to God—such as lust, bitterness, or dissatisfaction—take their place. Thanksgiving pushes back the wave of discontentment from earthly troubles with the larger reality of blessings in Christ. Gratitude grows us and guards us.

Gritty gratitude gives thanks in all circumstances because it depends on God's faithfulness and goodness, not on things being easy or having what we want. Most of us wait to give thanks until we have blessings in hand or think things have settled down, but the Bible puts thankful trust first. Don't wait to give thanks until you're happy about circumstances. Don't dwell on what's missing in your life. Set your mind on God and give thanks for all He is and has done. Joy follows gratitude.

DISCOURAGEMENT AND WEAKNESS

Every week, if not every day, discouragements deflate us like a punctured ball. We feel the weight of our weakness. The last thing you need is someone coaching you to suck it up, try harder, pull yourself together, and turn things around. And yet, that's often the message given to us. But trusting in our own strength eventually burns us out. Putting on a happy face and gritting our teeth as we push through doesn't lighten the load or pick us up off the ground.

Where does David go when discouraged? When his soul bottoms out and sorrow takes over, how does he resist the darkness and hold on to light? He gives thanks. He thanks God not only after difficulties, but he does so in the midst of them.

Psalm 28 is a cry for strength when David feels weak. He sees himself caught in a pit. It seems like his enemies gained the upper hand. Imminent defeat hovers above him like an oppressive cloud. But he doesn't stay there. He falls back on his two supports: prayer and thanksgiving. He asks God for victory but also for strength to keep going. Even as he waits, he preaches truth to his soul by assuring himself God hears his prayers. God will not abandon him.

David gives thanks before deliverance, even when fear and trembling dominate his emotions. "The LORD is my strength and my shield; in him my heart trusts, and I am helped; my heart exults, and with my song I give thanks to him" (Ps. 28:7). His circumstances haven't changed. There's no blessing received or desired outcome guaranteed. Tomorrow's situation might be the same as today. But David gives thanks to God. God will strengthen and sustain him. God hasn't abandoned him but will continue to help him.

Whatever you're walking through, God has not changed. He is still our helper and strength. By giving thanks for who He is, and reviving our weary soul by recalling God's faithfulness, thanks leads the way to trust and trust leads the way to hope. God's people push back the fears and sorrows pressing against us through thanksgiving (see Pss. 9; 30; 35:17–18, 27–28). As our gratitude list grows, so does our confidence in God's commitment to us.

DISTANCE FROM GOD

Maybe the hardest trial to endure is God's absence. When it feels like God is present, we can endure anything. But when it appears like He has hidden the warmth of His face, even the smallest trials seem unbearable.

Thanksgiving isn't only a defensive weapon helping us combat temptation or discouragement. Through thanksgiving we know, rest in, and worship God. Throughout the Bible, God's people pursue intimacy with God by giving thanks.

A repeated line throughout the Psalms thanks God for His steadfast love. "Oh give thanks to the LORD, for he is good, for his steadfast love endures forever!" (Ps. 106:1; see also 100:5; 118:1; 136:1). We praise what we delight in, and thanksgiving slows us down to see and enjoy it all the more. David gives thanks to God for His goodness and love. The act of considering and thanking God warms his heart toward Him.

The enemy wants to leverage our spiritual wilderness to whisper lies about God's character or purposes. When we give thanks, we counter his punches and say, "Not so fast." Giving thanks stirs up the truth about who God is to combat the questions and fears sprouting in our heart. Reflecting on God leads to rejoicing in Him. Thanksgiving knits our heart to God through the specifics we have to thank Him for. I pray this book helps you experience God's nearness and goodness.

JOYLESSNESS

We were made for joy. We won't feel right, at rest, or at peace until we have it. Because of this God-designed desire for joy, we never stop looking for it.

The problem is that we look in the wrong places. Rather than returning to God to find joy rooted in a satisfying, infinite joy-giver, we turn to the finite, disappointing, and deceiving things of the earth (idols). We find something shiny, some siren calling out to us with an offer to make us happy or satisfy our desires. We bite down on the hook only to realize we've been tricked. The idol fails us. The disappointment sets in and the emptiness widens. The desire for joy isn't met and it doesn't go away.

Like peanut butter and jelly, joy and thanksgiving go together. The ones who practice thanksgiving enjoy the by-product of joy. We enter His presence with praise, and in His presence we find joy (Ps. 16:11; 1 Thess. 5:16–18).

Thanksgiving changes us. It makes us happier. It offers us joy, not merely in the act of giving thanks and not only in the stuff we give thanks for, but in how it leads us to better know the Giver. Thanksgiving zooms in on the generous, loving, trustworthy, faithful heart of God.

Returning to Philippians 4, Paul encourages the church to rejoice, which means to take joy in something. "Rejoice in the Lord always; again I will say, rejoice ... do not be anxious about anything, but in everything by prayer and supplication with thanksgiving let your requests be made known to God. And the peace of God, which surpasses all understanding, will guard your hearts and your minds in Christ Jesus" (vv. 4–7). Joy flows to us when we wade in the river of thanksgiving. We find joy and peace by drawing near to God through thanksgiving and trust, believing He is what our thirsty soul needs.

David echoes Paul by rooting our joy in giving thanks. "Oh come, let us sing to the LORD; let us make a joyful noise to the rock of our salvation! Let us come into his presence with thanksgiving; let us make a joyful noise to him with songs of praise!" (Ps. 95:1–2). Then in 107:8–9, he adds, "Let them thank the LORD for his steadfast love, for his wondrous works to the children of man! For he satisfies the longing soul, and the hungry soul he fills with good things." We all look for joy. Thanksgiving points us in the direction it can be found. Our spirits lift as our eyes look up.

A DEFENSIVE AND OFFENSIVE WEAPON

Thanksgiving equips us to battle sin and struggles, including anxiety, lust, discontentment, fear, doubt, pride, and despair. Throughout this book we'll consider other sources and symptoms of ingratitude, such as busyness, entitlement, or complaining.

These are normal, ongoing struggles in the Christian life. If you identify with them, this book is for you. Gratitude isn't only a mountaintop experience. It's for anyone in the shadowy valley where the sun's warmth feels like a distant memory. God knows and understands what you're experiencing. And while thanksgiving isn't a magic wand to wave at surging emotions or daunting trials, through it we find joy and rest by shifting our eyes onto God.

Thanksgiving also produces righteous fruit, like joy, peace, trust, contentment, hope, and faith. Giving thanks is at the heart of a thriving faith in God. It's not a bonus, like heated car seats. It's not an optional spiritual rhythm we add on when life seems great. It's a necessary, daily, central practice to maintain worship and trust in life's ups and downs.

By finding reasons to give thanks, we uproot lingering discontentment. As we connect blessings to God as the source, our faith is fueled by knowing He's present and active. By expressing thanksgiving, it allows time for gratitude to deepen and push out grumbling from our heart. And as we reflect on God through thanksgiving, we know Him better.

Giving thanks won't remove all temptation. But as we consider the Bible's teachings on thanksgiving and make time to practice it, we'll experience its value firsthand through a deepened relationship with God. Thanksgiving offers God's people a way to know, trust, and rest in Him. By looking up and giving thanks, grumblers become grateful, and the grouchy find joy.

Putting It into Practice

HERE ARE SEVERAL WAYS TO PRACTICE GIVING THANKS. TRY ONE OR TWO THAT WORK FOR YOU.

1. Do the Gratitude Challenge in the appendix.
2. Build gratitude into your prayer life by thanking God at the beginning of your prayers.
3. Read a passage of Scripture and look for things you notice about the person and work of God. Give thanks in return.
4. Testify to God's goodness by sharing with one person a day something God has done that you're thankful for.
5. When eating with friends or family, ask everyone to share one thing they're thankful for.
6. Help children in your life develop gratitude to God by giving thanks. Ask them about good things in their life and who they come from. Help them to trace things to God.
7. You can find many good ideas online for incorporating thanksgiving into a craft or project—such as a Thanksgiving tree—to make it fun and memorable.

8. Write down personal or group prayer requests and record ways God answered prayers. Give thanks when it happens and when you look back on this list.

9. Go for a walk and give thanks to God for what you see in creation.

10. Find songs or written prayers of thanksgiving and sing or read through them.

11. Pick one attribute of God to study for a month. Find Bible verses related to that attribute. Read them and then give thanks to God for who He is.

CHAPTER 4

RECOGNIZE. REFLECT. RECEIVE.

I f only good intentions automatically led to good results. I might want to save money, but until I say no to buying gadgets and books, I'll keep busting our budget. How many times have you *said* you wanted to eat better, diet, exercise, pray more, or learn a new skill? How often have you started something—or thought about starting—only to give up after a couple days?

To change our habits for the long haul, we need training.

A couple years ago, my wife and I wanted to run a 5K race. Neither of us had any running experience, and I don't even enjoy running. I assumed Proverbs 28:1 warned us against running for no reason: "the wicked flee when no one pursues." For exercise, I'd rather play a sport, like basketball, tennis, or TV bingeing.

Since we began this endeavor with no running experience, we did a "couch to 5K" program. We needed a training strategy to alter our habits and prep us for the race, but we wanted realistic steps for the average person. If you've never done this routine, it starts you at level "couch potato" and over time boosts your endurance to run a 5K. Day 1 is a breeze. We walked for five minutes and that was it. But the next day it adds running for one minute, then two, then five, and before long you're running for miles at a time.

A program like this not only builds your muscles and endurance, but you also develop a *habit* of running. Every day or two, we laced up the sneakers, stretched our aging bodies, popped in headphones, and ran outside in the fresh air. Over time we could run faster for longer, our muscles didn't ache, and our lungs didn't burn like fire. Running became more natural and it felt less like a chore.

This is one example of the power of training to change our habits and develop sustainable practices. We need legs on our good intentions if we want different results. The same is true with giving thanks. Besides knowing it's biblical or beneficial, we need recalibrated rhythms.* Our convictions need help from our habits if we want lasting change.

In this chapter, we'll first consider two common roadblocks to thanksgiving. Busyness and distraction suffocate gratitude. These are the bad habits getting in gratitude's way. The second part will move from the problem to the solution. It's the "how to" section teaching us to recognize and receive God's gifts.

---

* We also need endurance. During trials, we might want to give thanks but emptiness or weariness make thanksgiving difficult. In chapter 9, we'll consider how to fight for gratitude and endurance in a valley.

DIAGNOSIS: TWO AILMENTS

Busyness

Our lives are full. Or at least our calendars are. Most people run at an unsustainable and unhealthy pace. We hurry from one thing to the next. We don't just run errands, we're run by them. Busyness pushes us.[1] It puts our head down into a steering wheel, desk, phone, or a computer screen and shouts: "Work harder and faster." Living this way forms tunnel vision. We only see what needs to be done or what's next on the agenda. This is true at our jobs, in the home, and in the car.

This kind of myopia narrows our sight, and we miss opportunities for gratitude. When we're looking down at our work or ahead on the road, physically present but mentally absent, we miss out on life. We don't see the gifts, abundance, and provision around us. We can't perceive God's hand in hard circumstances. God seems absent or uninvolved because we're not looking for Him. Our attention gravitates to calendars and lists rather than what God said in His Word or shows us in His world. Adele Calhoun explains:

> We can get so busy doing urgent things and so preoccupied with what comes next that we don't experience *now*. Afraid of being late, we rush from the past to the future. The present moment becomes a crack between what we did and what we have yet to do. It is virtually lost to us. We don't get to our futures any faster if we hurry. And we certainly don't become better people in haste. More likely than not, the faster we go the less we become.[2]

Busyness leaves no room for gratitude. It blinds us and burns us out.

Distraction

Related to busyness is distraction. We distract ourselves with busyness. Busyness drives us through the day like an overbearing boss, and distractions fill up any spare moments. When we have a few moments of downtime, we don't rejuvenate with rest, personal relationships, or life-giving activities. We gawk at glowing screens.[3]

This happens at restaurants, dinner tables, church, on dates, in school, and when riding in the car together. We are around one another, but not present with one another. We are in God's world, but not awake to the world. As fast as any gunslinger from the West, I snatch my phone and bring it up for a glance with the smallest window of free time. While waiting in a checkout line, drive-thru, or even just a stoplight, I feel the urge to distract myself or make sure I'm not missing anything. Like an itch needing to be scratched, my phone beckons for attention from my pocket.

Even when we're not staring at screens, we passively fill our minds with noise: music, podcasts, audiobooks, or radio. We rarely think proactively or deeply about spiritual truths, wisdom learned, or God's blessings. Many lack joy, wonder, meaningful friendships, excitement, and hope. Everything seems urgent but few things seem significant.

These are the blinking indicators of a busy, distracted life.

And on this parched ground the seeds of gratitude can't take root. Jon Bloom warns us about the danger of distraction:

> Lots of experts are talking about the negative effects this is having on us. Many of us feel it: the buzzing brain, the attention atrophy, the diminishing tolerance for reading, especially reading books.
>
> We're becoming conditioned to distraction, and it's harming our ability to listen and think carefully, to be still, to pray, and to meditate. Which means it is a spiritual danger, an evil from which we need God's deliverance (Matthew 6:13).[4]

If busyness squeezes out gratitude, distraction stiff-arms it. Opportunities for thanksgiving come close but we reject them by turning our attention to something else. Our eyes can't spot objects we could give thanks for because of our tunnel vision. Our minds don't process our surroundings or reflect on things we've experienced because they are preoccupied.

Like most doctor visits, this diagnosis might be a little embarrassing or painful. But unless we see what's harming us, we'll never change. In the next section, I move from diagnosis to prescription. To grow in gratitude, replace busyness and distraction with attentiveness and presence. Be where you are rather than being worried about where you're headed. Put down the device, look up, and notice the world.

PRESCRIPTION: SEEING AND RECEIVING

In *Liturgy of the Ordinary*, Tish Warren writes, "As busy, practical, hurried, and distracted people, we develop habits of inattention and miss these tiny theophanies in our day. But if we were fully alive and whole, no pleasure would be too ordinary or common-place to stir up adoration."[5] As we live present to the moment, the people, and our place, we can recognize, reflect on, and receive God's gifts. He scattered them everywhere for us to unwrap and enjoy.

We need training on grateful seeing. If you want to build up body muscle and lift more weights, you start small and get your reps in. The more often you lift, the more weight you can lift. Strengthen your gratitude muscles by starting small, getting your reps in, and making it a habit. Over time, you'll get stronger and stronger until you can lift praises like a spiritual Arnold Schwarzenegger.

We'll consider three ways to respond to God's gifts. Think of these as handrails to guide you up the stairs of gratitude. Recognize. Reflect. Receive.

Recognize what's around you.

Reflect on its significance and source.

Receive it gratefully as a gift and rejoice.

Recognize

To recognize something, we identify and acknowledge what we observe. We see things in such a way we can appreciate them. To give thanks, we note reasons for giving thanks.

The very first thing we must do is open our eyes, look around, and notice the glorious but groaning, beautiful, and broken world we live in. See. Be present. Through paying attention to the world, we discern God's provision and activity. We also do this when we open God's Word. Don't skim it; study it. Be on the lookout for God in it. Identify His promises, blessings, works, attributes, and truths.

The journey to joy and gratitude begins by recognizing God in His world and Word. We must see the gifts we ignore, presume, or take for granted that have become white noise. Charles Spurgeon wrote:

> I want to urge you, dear friends, to observe the goodness
> of God carefully for your souls' good. There is a great
> difference between eyes and no eyes. Yet, many have eyes
> and yet see not. God's goodness flows before them, but
> they say, "Where is it?" They breathe it but ask, "Where
> is it?" They sit at the table and are fed upon it. They
> wear it upon their limbs. It is in the very beating of their
> hearts, and yet they wonder, "Where is it?" Do not be so
> blind.... Let us know the Lord and consider His great
> goodness.[6]

Eyes that see give us a key to unlock a door to thanksgiving. Before we can say thanks to God, we must have something to thank Him for. We cannot give thanks if we're not thankful for anything in particular.

One book that taught me this was *One Thousand Gifts* by Ann Voskamp.[7] She retells her story with a running commentary on her dare to list one thousand gifts from God. "In naming that which is right before me, that which I'd otherwise miss, the invisible becomes visible."[8] Stuff she didn't give a second glance before became cherished gifts. "The art of deep seeing makes gratitude possible. And it is the art of gratitude that makes joy possible."[9] Follow the logic of her sentence in reverse. There is no joy without gratitude, and gratitude is impossible apart from "the art of deep seeing."

> **Until we put away distractions, slow down, and pause to look for His faithfulness, we'll run past the world with eyes blindfolded to God. If we bury our heads in the sand, we cannot blame God for the view.**

Through seeing—intentionally living present to the world full of God's fingerprints—we discover the pleasures and joys God placed around us. We can even recognize His hand and plan in difficult circumstances so we endure and trust. But until we put away distractions, slow down, and pause to look for His faithfulness, we'll run past the world with eyes blindfolded to God. If we bury our heads in the sand, we cannot blame God for the view.

Did you pick up this book wondering why you're not more grateful, hoping for more of the joy gratitude infuses into life? If so, ask yourself if you live in such a way as to recognize the gifts around you or if you walk by them, missing or ignoring them. Do you live with your antenna turned on so God's gifts, activity, provision, providence, or presence registers on your radar? Is your head up and eyes open? Are you hurried and distracted or present and interested?

Reflect

Recognizing God's gifts is the first stop on the road to thanksgiving. Not only do we recognize something but we reflect on it. We observe, and then we consider. Recognition involves not just seeing something but processing what you're seeing.

Here's an example. As I write this, I'm working at my favorite local coffee shop. Looking around, I'm in a room with people of various ages, wooden tables, hot and cold drinks, and bookshelves. One entire wall is a large glass window, filling the room with sunlight. It opens views to the street lined with small businesses, antique shops, local restaurants, and people strolling along the sidewalk. My eyes catch the beauty of the blue sky, the stately green trees standing on our historic square, and pink flowers in large planters. Aromas of espresso, frothy milk, and roasted beans fill the air. My black coffee warms my body and keeps caffeine coursing through my veins.

I'm recognizing what's around me. And as I *reflect* on them, I realize their preciousness and it sets me up to *receive* them as gifts (our next section).

Moving past recognition into reflection, I'm thankful for a spot full of fellow community members. Some meet for business purposes, including developing and improving our city. Others meet for conversation and friendship. Fellow believers meet to encourage one another, talk about the Bible, and pray together. Life happens here, and I'm thankful for it.

The sights and smells remind me God filled our world with color, beauty, diversity, purpose, fragrances, and shade. God created these things, upholds them, and delights in them. He gives them for our good and our enjoyment. The more I reflect on these things, the more they tell me about their Maker (Rom. 1:20; Ps. 19:1–6). His heart is kind and His gifts are good.

I find a similar pleasure reflecting on—and sipping—my coffee, contemplating how it reaches my table from bean to barista. God filled the earth with trees (Gen. 1:29), both for mankind's provision and pleasure (Gen. 2:9). The coffee plant ripens little cherry-like fruits containing seeds, or coffee beans. In one of humanity's shining moments, someone in history used their God-given creativity to turn the seed into a beverage. They discovered if you roasted the seed, ground it up, and ran hot water through it, you'd have the most magnificent drink. (Thank you, whoever you were.)

Returning to the present, farmers around the world grow coffee. People plant seeds, care for the trees, and harvest the cherries. Others process and dry the beans. At some point it's exported, roasted, and packaged. My local barista scoops it into the coffee maker, adds hot water, and flips the switch on. They pour it in a cup and hand it to me with a smile. As I sit down to drink it, I savor it and find enjoyment.

I'm thankful for the people and process of turning a tree, thousands of miles away, into a tasty beverage. I'm thankful to a generous, joy-giving God for making the world full of wonders and gifts like this for us.

Now you might not spend that much time staring into your coffee, considering its source, but when we reflect on ordinary things, we see them in a different light. Lackluster items tossed to the side become shiny gems tucked away in our pocket.

Receive

The more we reflect on what we recognize, the more we're set up to receive it as a gift. At the heart of thanksgiving is receiving. We not only take a gift in our hands; we realize it's given.

Humility allows us to live a given, received life. That's very different from living with a sense of entitlement and pride. Pride says I earned and accomplished this. Life is understood in terms of earning. Entitlement says I deserve everything I have, and then some. Blessings are viewed as rights and demanded. Due to our pride and sense of entitlement, we greedily gobble up blessings without recognizing them as gifts.

A humble, dependent gratitude confesses we've been given more than we deserve or have earned, and we've been helped and blessed by many along the way. Life is seen here as a gift. In his writings, Wendell Berry locates "the given life" at the heart of how we live as creatures with gratefulness. Ragan Sutterfield writes:

> For Berry, thanksgiving is fully living into our givenness—it is the acceptance that our life is a miracle. To be thankful is to take pleasure in our existence and in the things that make existence possible. "In this pleasure," writes Berry, "we experience and celebrate our dependence and our gratitude, for we are living from mystery, from creatures we did not make and powers we cannot comprehend."[10]

The practice of recognizing and receiving gifts requires crucial shifts: from pride to humility, from grasping for the role of

Creator to resting in our role as creatures, from viewing things around us as exploitable and expendable resources to gifts we receive and revel in, and from asserting our independence to admitting our dependence on and need for others.

Recognition, reflection, and reception often move us to feeling thankful because they make an impression on us. This won't always be the case. We can't force our feelings and don't have to wait on them to give thanks. But the more we experience something as valuable, the more likely we are to say thanks and live gratefully.

Seeing Reasons to Give Thanks*

Gratitude will always be challenging to come by if we can't recognize God's gifts. For those who have developed the skill of seeing, this is more natural. For others, this might be a stretch. If that's the case, don't give up. The practice of recognizing takes training, but all discipline gets easier and becomes more beneficial the longer we stick with it. Commit to looking for reasons to give thanks this week.

> [C. S.] Lewis reminds us that "one must walk before one can run. . . . [We] shall not be able to adore God on the highest occasions if we have learned no habit of doing

---

* You could look at many biblical examples of thanksgiving and trace out what this looks like. For example, in Romans 1:8, Paul *recognizes* their belief in God, he *reflects* on how their belief and obedience demonstrates God's work in them, and he *receives* it as something only God could do, which leads to giving thanks. See also Pss. 75:1; 79:13; 107:1–2; Dan. 2:23; Matt. 15:36; Luke 17:16; Acts 28:15; Rom. 14:6; 2 Cor. 9:15; Eph. 1:15–16; 1 Tim. 1:12.

so on the lowest. At best, our faith and reason will tell us that he is adorable but we shall not have *found* him so."

These tiny moments of beauty in our days train us in the habits of adoration and discernment. And the pleasure and sensuousness of our gathered worship teach us to look for and receive these small moments in our days. Together, they train us in the art of noticing and of reveling in God's goodness and artistry.[11]

Walk before you run. Enjoy the little moments. Savor small gifts. Hold on to anything God teaches you or does for you.

In this chapter, we considered how we might recognize, reflect on, and receive God's gifts. The next chapter transitions us from acknowledging gifts to appreciating the Giver. We'll learn more about what to be grateful for, and where to point our gratitude.

Putting It into Practice

RECORD

As the hymn says, "Count your blessings, name them one by one. Count your many blessings, see what God has done!"[12] Recording blessings reinforces their value and files the memory away. As I write things down, I say thanks, stir up thanks, and save my reasons for giving thanks so I can revisit them later. Just like we take pictures to not lose important moments, we write things down to not lose important thoughts and experiences.

We trust our brain's ability to keep details more than we should. When you go to a restaurant and your waiter or waitress takes everyone's order without jotting it down, you know someone's food is coming back wrong. Every time I run to the grocery store I forget something unless I've made a list. I assume I'll remember because there are less than ten things, but to my wife's dismay, my mind goes blank and I forget something (usually the most important item). If that's the case with a grocery list of seven items from ten minutes prior, how can I expect my mind to recall God's gifts and works over weeks, months, and years?

Unless you put on paper an answered prayer or what God did, you'll likely forget it. Record in order to recall. The most common way of recording something is to write it down, either on paper, in a journal, on your phone, or on your computer. I have a journal where I write things down but I also use a note-keeping app on my phone and computer. Record what you see in God's Word, a list of things you're thankful for, prayer requests and answered prayers, or ways you see God at work. See every line as a chance to give thanks to God.

Review the list as one way to remember God's work in your life and what He's taught you. Use these things as conversation starters at the dinner table or in the car.

Before closing this book and moving on to something else, decide how you will start a thanksgiving list. Where will you write down what you're thankful to God for and what you're recognizing around you? Try having a time of the day you do this (like before bed) or commit to writing down a specific number of things each day (such as five).

Recognize. Reflect. Receive. Then record and review.

WRITE A THANKSGIVING PRAYER

Putting a prayer on paper (or computer) can help you process how you might tell God thanks. Try writing out your own thanksgiving prayer. It doesn't have to be perfectly written, but try to write at least half a page telling God why you're thankful to Him and what you're learning about Him. This is different from the prior application because you're doing more than listing reasons to give thanks. Here you're telling God thanks in a written prayer.

CHAPTER 5

LOOK AROUND
AND LOOK UP

I spent last Christmas with my wife, almost two-year-old daughter, and mother-in-law. After waking up, we first opened stockings to get the holiday juices flowing. Stockings are the appetizers of Christmas. You enjoy it, but it's a foretaste of better things ahead. After coffee and cinnamon rolls, we moved on to bigger gifts. My wife bought me clothes (always trying to better my style), camping gear, and shoes with the colors and logo of the New England Patriots. Because I live in the Indianapolis area, church members extend patience and love, not to mention unity in diversity, for my Patriots fandom. My mother-in-law assembled a foodie box with the five food groups: dark chocolate, Cape Cod Potato Chips, maple syrup, beef jerky, and coffee.

My toddler didn't get me anything, and I forgave her. She was, no surprise, the center of attention for the holidays. Though I'm the youngest of four siblings and have been the "baby" of the family my whole life, I've adjusted to her stealing the show from me.

The Christmas before she was only eleven months old. Our expectations for how magical Christmas would be with a baby smashed as quickly as the ornaments she knocked off the tree. But this year proved different. She opened her gifts, expressed emotion, said thanks, and played with her toys. Among the many gifts we gave her—and no, I don't give Santa the credit—were a kid's backpack, clothes, a bit of chocolate (I passed on my dessert cravings), Mickey Mouse books, stuffed animals, and toys.

Opening gifts can be a joyful, bonding experience. Even at her age, she's aware gifts don't appear out of nowhere. We water those seeds of understanding by connecting the dots from the gift to the giver. We told her before and after opening a present who it was from. If we gave it to her, she would tell us thank you. If it was from someone else, she might say thanks for a video we could text to a family member. I didn't go over the top by demanding she thank someone or I would return everything. We simply encouraged gratitude where we could. We taught her by joining thankfulness *for* a gift and thankfulness *to* a giver.

CHRISTIAN GRATITUDE

I need that lesson firmed up in my own heart. Behind every good gift is a kind giver. Thankfulness takes us from the object received to its source.

In our last chapter, we learned about the value of *recognizing* God's gifts. Unless we see reasons for gratitude, we'll never give thanks. You can't feel grateful for gifts you don't know exist. You can't thank God for lessons you haven't learned. But feeling grateful should lead to another step: thanking someone.

Thankfulness for *something* leads us to thankfulness to *someone*.

Self-focused gratitude grabs on to the gift alone. Biblical gratitude wraps its big arms around the recipient, the gift, and the giver. It embraces gift and giver as es-

What we're thankful *for* points us to who we're thankful *to*.

sential parts of our joy. The step of recognizing gifts is essential, but incomplete. Thanksgiving isn't naming off blessings, though it might start there. It affirms blessings in our life to appreciate the person who gave them. What we're thankful *for* points us to who we're thankful *to*.

COMPANION PLANTS AND CHRISTIAN PRACTICES

I'm no master gardener, but in my small-scale gardening I've learned about companion planting. Some flowers, vegetables, and herbs grow better together. They don't just tolerate one another; they encourage one another's health and fruitfulness. But some plants can't grow together. One steals nutrients, blocks the sun, or entices pests that hinder the growth of other plants.

The same is true in our life. Faith, humility, and thankfulness are companion practices, supporting and sustaining one another. As one increases, so do the others. But unbelief and boasting choke out the tiniest seedlings of thankfulness. Whereas humility and gratitude feed off each other, gratitude and pride cannot coexist in proximity. Either we'll view ourselves as the source of good things and take the credit, or we'll acknowledge God behind everything we have and redirect the glory to Him. As our lives center on God, gratitude grows. When self-focus sprouts and spreads, gratefulness withers.

The more we're convinced God is the Maker, Giver, and Provider of all things, the more this primes us to view everything as an opportunity for praise.[1] Nancy DeMoss Wolgemuth writes, "It is only by recognizing that our blessings have a single source—a real, personal, living, and loving Giver—that gratitude begins its transformation into authentic, *Christian* gratitude: *recognizing and expressing appreciation for the benefits we have received from God and others.*"[2]

Biblical thanksgiving pegs God as the primary source of anything and everything good. "Every good gift and every perfect gift is from above, coming down from the Father of lights, with whom there is no variation or shadow due to change" (James 1:17). The gifts around us aren't a matter of luck, fortune, how the cookie crumbles, or the way the cards land. They're from God.* Faith fuels gratitude because it pinpoints God as the fount from whom all blessings flow. And gratitude increases our faith as we see and taste His goodness firsthand.

---

* One contemporary challenge to gratitude is the pervasive naturalism of our culture. As recent books have demonstrated, a disenchanted naturalism pervades our Western society—including the church—so our default way of relating to the world is through natural causes and explanations. It puts us in an "immanent frame," making transcendent interruptions from beyond seem unlikely. This affects gratitude because our way of perceiving blessings is to consider the earthly, natural cause apart from God's providence and provision. See *How (Not) to Be Secular* by James K. A. Smith, *Our Secular Age* edited by Collin Hansen, *Recapturing the Wonder* by Mike Cosper, and *Disruptive Witness* by Alan Noble.

Since anything we have ultimately comes from God—even things we obtain through hard work—gratitude chokes out pride and boasting. "What do you have that you did not receive? If then you received it, why do you boast as if you did not receive it?" (1 Cor. 4:7). Lift-

The gifts around us aren't a matter of luck, fortune, how the cookie crumbles, or the way the cards land. They're from God.

ing our hands in praise to God should replace patting ourselves on the back.

In the rest of this chapter, I want to bridge the gap between things we're thankful for and the One we're thankful to. We'll walk through five categories of God's blessings: God's common grace, God's creation, God's providence and provision, God's gifts of grace in Christ, and God Himself. (These don't exhaust God's blessings, but they provide clearly marked fountains to drink from in order to savor God and His gifts.)

GOD'S COMMON GRACE

Christians and non-Christians alike have access to God's common grace. "Common" might not sound like a big compliment, but it conveys the audience, not the quality of the gift. They're experienced by being in the world originally created by God as good.[3] The sun shines and the rain falls on the just and the unjust (Matt. 5:45). They differ from gifts of "special grace" or "saving grace" given only in Jesus.

With our first breath in the morning, the blessings from God tally up. The creaturely benefits call for gratitude to the Creator. Which of these can you thank God for?

- Sleep. Even better, sleep under a roof on a bed with warm covers.
- Active minds and bodies.
- Running water, plumbing, hot showers, and a toothbrush for morning breath (even if you're not grateful for brushed teeth, your family and coworkers will be).
- A refrigerator and the food inside.
- A job, including the money it provides and the opportunity to use your experiences and skills.
- People you care about and who care about you.

We might contribute to these things, but apart from God's generosity and kindness, we would have none of them. Give thanks.

GOD'S CREATION

The Apostles' Creed confesses belief in "God, the Father Almighty, Maker of heaven and earth." God stuffed our planet with wonders, pleasures, and blessings. If God is the Maker of all things, our world offers no shortage of reasons to give thanks. Nature dazzles us with glimpses of God's majesty and might.[4] In Psalm 95, the psalmist looks to God's creation for thanksgiving: "Let us come into his presence with thanksgiving; let us make a joyful noise to him with songs of praise! . . . In his hand are the depths of the earth; the heights of the mountains are his also. The sea is his, for he made it, and his hands formed the dry land" (vv. 2, 4–5).

Creation not only reveals God; it praises God. God aimed for creation to stir awe in us so thanksgiving would erupt from us. First we say "Wow!" because of it and then we say "Thank You!" for it. The Creator's glory invites the creature's gratitude.

- A world full of beauty to enjoy, from the sky's colorful hues at dusk, to the sun's relentless glow, to shade-giving and fruit-bearing trees (just try a Honey Crisp apple).
- The unique skills, gifts, personalities, and experiences God gives people and the resources filling the earth, which we cultivate and steward.
- We take in glorious sights, but also our ears enable us to hear music that moves us. We pick up scents with our noses (some delightful—like fresh Play-Doh—and some pungent), tastes on our tongues, and the sensation of a cool breeze on our face or the sun's rays warming our skin.
- As we eat, we acknowledge that God provides the food, seasonings, and liquids for our nourishment, strength, and pleasure (depending on the cook).

Creation grabs our attention, but it does so to point us to a bigger and better Creator. What in creation can you ponder and praise God for?

GOD'S PROVIDENCE AND PROVISION

Through eyes of faith we interpret God's activity around us in His providence and for us in His provision. God's providence refers to His sovereign governance and oversight of our world. The guiding influence in our universe isn't fate, luck, or "the force." It's the always good, absolutely wise, and intimately personal God.

Part of God's providence comes through in His provision. God provides jobs, homes, finances, friends, and healthy bodies, to name a few things. God answers prayer. He supplies our needs. He delivers. You earned the paycheck, but would you have the job opportunity, a healthy body and brain so you can work, or the skills apart from God's direction and blessing?

When Nebuchadnezzar reigned as king, Daniel gave thanks to God for both His providence in where He places people and His provision in explaining the dream (see Dan. 2:20–23). God's providence and provision, though mysterious, led to praise.

- Recall when God answered prayer, supplied a need, or delivered you from trouble.
- Can you see God's faithful and kind hand at work recently or throughout your life?
- What are blessings given to you? How do they point to God's providence and provision?

GOD'S GRACE THROUGH CHRIST

Whereas God spreads common grace blessings on both believers and unbelievers, there are other blessings only those united to Christ by faith receive. They are peculiar to God's redeemed people. These gifts of grace, purchased by Christ's blood, are the greatest of gifts and produce the deepest gratitude. They were costly for Jesus and they prove priceless for us. As Charles Spurgeon said:

> If you must have a little list of what He has given you, ponder the following: He has given you a name and place among His people. He has given you rights and nature of His sons. He has given you the complete forgiveness of all your sins, and you have it now. He has given you a robe of righteousness which you are wearing now. He has given you a superlative loveliness in Christ Jesus. He has given you access to Him and acceptance at the mercy seat. He has given you this world and the worlds to come. He has given you all that He has. He has given you His own Son, and how shall He now refuse you anything? Oh, He has given as only God could.[5]

Nothing flushes out ingratitude, discontentment, and unhappiness like the gospel. Nancy DeMoss Wolgemuth writes, "Undeniable guilt, plus undeserved grace, should equal unbridled gratitude."[6]

Jesus saves us from our sin. Jesus satisfies us in our emptiness. Jesus sustains us in our weariness. He squelches our fears and covers our shame. He shelters us in His love and shields us by His power. Jesus sanctifies and matures us by the Spirit's powerful presence and sends us out on a purposeful mission. What we have in the person and work of Jesus fills our life with grace and floods us with gratitude.

In his famous chapter on Christ's resurrection victory, Paul rejoices in the hope of eternal, resurrected life through Jesus.

"But thanks be to God, who gives us the victory through our Lord Jesus Christ" (1 Cor. 15:57; see also Rom. 6:17). Victory through Jesus prompts thanks for Jesus.

In the gospel, you encounter a bottomless well of God's gracious gifts. If you want to avoid straying from gratitude, stick close to Christ.

- Where would you be apart from God's grace and mercy?
- As you consider the weight of your sin before Christ, and its chains of shame and regret, how does forgiveness and freedom through Jesus make you grateful?
- How has the Holy Spirit worked in you, both at conversion but also over the years? How has He strengthened, assisted, and sustained you?
- Where have you tasted God's power, deliverance, love, comfort, presence, or blessing?
- What promises belong to you as God's son or daughter?

GOD

When we think about or learn about God, we find reasons to give thanks. God's deeds prompt thanksgiving. God's attributes and character behind His works also promote thanksgiving. To get specific in our thanksgiving to God, we must grow in our knowledge of Him.

By increasing our knowledge of God—learned and experienced—we make faith deposits. These investments pay off with the dividends of gratitude and joy. While acquiring general data can puff up, whether *Jeopardy!* facts or biblical trivia answers, the knowledge of God changes us. Knowing God doesn't just fill our heads with information but it produces transformation. It shouldn't roll over us like water off a duck. Seeing God leads to savoring God, which leads to responding to Him.

We praise and thank God for who He is and what He's done. Through revering God, we rejoice in God. God's people give thanks, not only to God but also for God. "I will give to the LORD the thanks due to his righteousness, and I will sing praise to the name of the LORD, the Most High" (Ps. 7:17; see also Ps. 75:1; Ezra 3:11; 1 Cor. 1:4).[7]

- How might you worship God in thanksgiving and praise for these attributes: mercy, love, kindness, faithfulness, wisdom and knowledge, holiness, righteousness, and patience?
- What are your favorite stories, chapters, or verses in the Bible? What do they tell you about God that incites thanksgiving?
- What has God done in the past and how has He proven His faithfulness?

CONNECTING OUR EYES TO OUR HEARTS

We'll soon return to how thanking God leads to communion with God (chapter 7). For now, I want the things we feel grateful *for* to lead us to the One we are thankful *to*. We need open eyes to recognize gifts, but we need open hearts to worship the Giver.

Sometimes giving thanks feels overwhelming because we don't know where to begin. We know God has done many things we should feel thankful for, but unless we get specific, we'll miss out on gratitude. The categories in this chapter provide a starting point. They help us identify God as the source of every good gift.

Though God is more important than His gifts, we don't need to demean His gifts. God gives us these things out of a heart full of love for us, both so we can enjoy what He provides and so we can better know Him through it. You shouldn't feel guilty for the thrill of unwrapping and delighting in a present on Christmas morning, nor should you feel guilty for receiving what God gives. But in both cases, rather than ignoring the Giver, enjoy the gift with the one who gave it by saying thanks.

Putting It into Practice

LOOK AROUND

After this chapter, pause to look around. What do you see and hear? What blessings and provision of God exist in front of you? Whether you're sitting in a room, outside, or reading from a café, take a moment to notice every little thing.

Walk through your house, church, office, or any other familiar space and let the things you see be opportunities to give thanks. Give thanks to God not only for the things you see, but more so for His kindness and faithfulness in the memories, stories, experiences, and relationships tied to those items. For example, if I see my kitchen table, I might thank God for the gift of food and flavor, that He provides and we don't go without eating, for the people we love who have sat around it, for good conversations among family or friends over a meal, or for that time we laughed through a joyful celebration or cried through a painful situation.

LOOK BACK

Reflect on your day or week and consider blessings you've experienced. Think through the categories in this chapter, using them as a springboard for giving thanks.

LOOK UP

Take time to contemplate where you can thank God. After looking around at the gifts you have and looking back at the gifts God has provided in the past, look up in thanksgiving as you recognize the source of these blessings.

CHAPTER 6

THANKFULNESS EXPRESSED

The phrase "It's the thought that counts" might work in some situations (like when my toddler "helps" put dishes away and somehow the forks end up next to the vinegar), but in most cases, it's not true. Having a grateful thought isn't the same as saying thank you.

Imagine you have a project at work. You invest a lot of time, mental energy, and sweat equity. After a few weeks, you finish the project and present it to your team. You crushed it. Your team dishes out handshakes, high fives, or fist bumps. You've got a little extra swagger in your step this day.

If that work impressed your boss, and he appreciated what you did, would you want to hear that from him, or is it okay if he *feels* appreciation but never says so? I'm guessing you'd like some affirmation for a job well done and for the many hours spent on it. Something. Anything. If you hear nothing but crickets, you might wonder if he noticed the work, or if he liked it. You'd be discouraged or frustrated if you never received a thank-you.

In your next one-on-one, you bring the project up and ask why he never gave you feedback. If he said, "I appreciated your work but never got around to telling you," it might relieve you to know what he thought, but it would sting since he didn't bother to say anything. You might even question the sincerity of his words. If he *really* liked it, wouldn't he have said something? Genuine gratitude leads to some expression of saying thanks.

The same would be true in someone's apartment or house. I'm no expert at cleaning. I'm better at tidying up and rearranging items from one room to a closet than I am at deep cleaning. (Several years in a college dorm and then living with single guys lowered my standard of cleanliness.) But if I put away dishes, swept the floors, picked up scattered toys, smell-checked my clothes and tossed the bad ones into the washer, and gave my best shot at deep-cleaning the bathroom, I'd want a thank-you. I bet you would want to hear that too. The simple "thank you" helps me know someone saw and appreciated what I did.

Thanksgiving includes something we're thankful for, someone we're thankful to, and saying thanks.

To give thanks, we must *give* thanks. It's a verb.

PUTTING THOUGHTS INTO WORDS

Without giving thanks to God for who He is and what He's done, there's something missing in our gratitude. Like cookies without the sugar, it's flat. C. S. Lewis writes, "I think we delight to praise what we enjoy because the praise not merely expresses but completes the enjoyment; it is its appointed consummation."[1] Unspoken gratitude is incomplete gratitude.

There's no short supply of Bible verses about verbalizing gratitude.[2] There are some things we should hold in, but thanksgiving isn't one of them. We can express giving thanks through praying, singing, or telling others what God has done.[3]

> Oh give thanks to the LORD; call upon his name;
>> make known his deeds among the peoples!
> Sing to him, sing praises to him;
>> tell of all his wondrous works! (Ps. 105:1–2)

> Let the redeemed of the LORD say so,
>> whom he has redeemed from trouble. . . .
> Let them thank the LORD for his steadfast love,
>> for his wondrous works to the children of man!
> And let them offer sacrifices of thanksgiving,
>> and tell of his deeds in songs of joy!
> (Ps. 107:2, 21–22)

> Through him [Jesus] then let us continually offer up
> a sacrifice of praise to God, that is, the fruit of lips that
> acknowledge his name. (Heb. 13:15)

When we consider God's grace in our life—the many deliverances, mighty deeds, and daily blessings—thanksgiving is fitting. The internal pressure of gratitude must go somewhere, and saying thank you releases it like built-up air in a pressure cooker.

BENEFITS OF SAYING THANKS

Pixar's movie *Inside Out* tells the story of emotions at work in a girl named Riley. The delightful film personifies several emotions to picture how they work together and against one another. They operate out of a control center in her mind. If a certain emotion (or character) touches memories or gets behind the control center, it directly affects Riley's actions. *Inside Out* draws connections from outward behaviors to internal influences.

Imagine we added two characters to the story. The first is a pleasant character named Gratitude. She's a yellow and orange color, glowing like the evening sun. When she walks into Headquarters, she brings out the best in everybody. The second character is a curmudgeonly killjoy known as Ingratitude. She's a pale grey color, and a looming rain cloud follows above her. When she walks into Headquarters, the mood changes and everyone avoids her.

We can either put gratitude or ingratitude behind the command post, but one of them will be there.

Because our heart always leans toward either gratitude or ingratitude, one of the two sits at the control center at all times. When Gratitude takes the helm, touching our memories and pushing the buttons on our heart, it leads to a specific set of thoughts, behaviors, words, and actions (as we'll see below). Joy joins her and they work together. When the more erratic Ingratitude gets her moment of power, an opposite set of behaviors show up, such as grumbling, fear, worry, discontentment, and bitterness. Anger slides up next to her.

While the Bible doesn't describe our behavior exactly like a Pixar movie, both press us to connect the relationship between what's at power inside of us and the corresponding behaviors that come out of us. When we choose to give thanks, we empower gratitude, putting it at the headquarters of our heart. Gratitude then not only does something in us, but it redirects our words, emotions, and actions. Unlike how *Inside Out* portrays Riley primarily as a passive vehicle, we have a large role in choosing which emotion or attitude sits in the power-seat of our lives. We can either put gratitude or ingratitude behind the command post, but one of them will be there.

In this section, we'll consider four effects and benefits of giving thanks.

It Gives Credit Where Credit Is Due

We should say thanks when something kindles our appreciation. I shared human examples earlier in the chapter, but this is also true with God.

When we give thanks, we affirm truths about God. We verbalize our experience of who God is and what He's done. When God is faithful, upholds us, or delivers us, it's both right and good to tell Him we're thankful. God is good, kind, holy, righteous, and steadfast in His love. If those things matter to you, acknowledge Him in thanksgiving. Thank Him for being God. Through thanksgiving, God gets the praise He deserves, and we get the benefit of considering and confessing the worthiness of the living God.

It Imprints Gratitude

Putting half-formed thoughts into words develops those thoughts. Charles Spurgeon commended thanksgiving in the following words: "Uttering the divine goodness is a great help to the memory of it. By teaching, we learn. By giving the truth expression, we deepen its impression upon our minds."[4] I might have a thankful thought, but too often it's short-lived. It stays small, unless it turns into thanking God. Something changes in me as I recognize a gift, reflect on its value, receive it, and relay my appreciation to God. It deepens and widens the gratitude, allowing it to stretch its elbows and find room to have a seat at the table of my heart.

When we take the time to express thanks, it's like sprinkling Miracle-Gro on our gratitude. Our gratitude grows with new life and vitality. Its roots deepen. We might have many fleeting emotions of gratefulness throughout a week, but unless thanksgiving seals them in our hearts, we'll forget them. If we continually forget reasons for gratitude—or our experience of gratitude—we'll assume we have little to thank God for. If our heart is devoid of gratitude because it never takes root, it won't remain empty or neutral. Ingratitude takes its place. Discontentment, bitterness, frustration, and jealousy will crop up. Guard your heart by stamping gratitude on it.

It Redirects Our Words and Deeds

Grumblers become grateful when our words of thanksgiving drown out our grumbling. Think of sinful responses of the tongue: criticizing, lying, gossiping, tearing down, murmuring.

By filling our conversation with thanksgiving, we hang up a "No Vacancy" sign alerting grumbling and complaining that they better look elsewhere. As Paul Tripp writes, "The longer praise is in our hearts and in our mouths the less time complaint has opportunity to dominate our words."[5]

Do you want to be known for griping, complaining, or whining? Do you want people to tune you out because they're tired of your negativity? None of us want that. No one says, "I really want to be one of those nagging, irritable people the next few years." But apart from a handful of natural optimists who see life in terms of rainbows and butterflies, we all drift toward grumbling. Sinful, crooked hearts fly to it like bugs to a light. Zap. Something intentional must be done to win our war of words.

In Ephesians 4:17, Paul kicks off a famous passage on our life in Christ. He admonishes us to put off vices (sins) *and* replace them with virtues, such as countering theft with honest work (4:22–24, 28). He then moves to how we speak. "Let no corrupting talk come out of your mouths, but only such as is good for building up, as fits the occasion, that it may give grace to those who hear" (4:29). He builds on this a few verses later. "Let there be no filthiness nor foolish talk nor crude joking, which are out of place, but instead let there be thanksgiving" (5:4; see also 5:20).

Bad language goes beyond cusswords causing your mom to blush. Paul instructs us to retune our words with notes of gratitude as the means to replace off-putting, discouraging language. Put off ungrateful speech not merely by willpower and discipline ("don't say it, don't say it, don't say it"), but by redirecting and seasoning your words with thanksgiving and grace. Put off ingratitude *and* put on gratitude. Put off ungrateful speech *by* putting on grateful speech. We cannot fulfill Paul's command to "do all things without grumbling" (Phil. 2:14) unless we instead are "giving thanks always and for everything" (Eph. 5:20).

When I speak out of anger, it's because things feel outside of my control or I fear what's taking place. Or I just want (demand) things to be easier. I don't like what my daughter is doing or that she's not listening. A decision at work inconveniences me. A trial frustrates me. Part of how I can level the anger fortified in my heart is pounding it with waves of gratitude.

Thank You, God, that You are in control rather than me.

Thank You, God, that You have good plans for me, even though I wouldn't choose this.

Thank You, God, that You are with me and will sustain me through this.

Thank You, God, that this is momentary and temporary.

That doesn't mean in a tense moment I don't feel anger heating up in my veins, but I want to be proactive. I tell my sinful emotions where they can go and what they can do rather than letting them push me around. As I give thanks, the tide starts to shift. Anger gives way to trust. Through voicing thanksgiving, my heart jumps on board. I put off angry words *by* voicing thanksgiving.

The same is true of my fear, worries, disappointment, whining, or grumbling. We not only replace murmuring speech through giving thanks but we counter the ungodly sentiments in our heart. Gary Thomas writes, "I like to think of thankfulness as God's 'spiritual air freshener.' It replaces the stale odor of resentment with clean, fresh-smelling air for the soul to breathe."[6]

We sometimes use candles or air fresheners to mask bad scents in my house. Candles overpower an unpleasant smell, but they don't eliminate it. Giving thanks is different. It might not completely eliminate the pungent odors of sin from the fibers of our heart, but it does more than cover them up. Gratitude gets into our anger, grumbling, and discontentment and starts to dissolve them. These things fade and get smaller as our sights of God get stronger and bigger. The anger isn't just momentarily covered up by gratitude; it's defused by gratitude (at least in part).

It Promotes Discipleship and Witness

A fourth benefit is that thanksgiving puts God on display before others. We encourage fellow believers and evangelize unbelievers through declaring who God is and what He's done.

The Bible often links thanksgiving with telling others about the deeds of God (Ps. 107:1, 21; Luke 2:38; 17:11–19). It glorifies God, helps us grow, and serves the good of those around us. Charles Spurgeon wrote, "If you abundantly talk of God's goodness, you are sure to benefit your neighbors. Many are comforted when they hear of God's goodness to your friends."[7] Our words influence. They can sap life from others or fan life into them. They can pull people into the ditch with us when we grumble or guide them along a path toward God through gratitude.

Parents teach their kids by telling them what's true and by reinforcing those truths through personal stories of thanksgiving

Our words influence. They can sap life from others or fan life into them. They can pull people into the ditch with us when we grumble or guide them along a path toward God through gratitude.

(see Deut. 4:9–14; 6:7; Pss. 78:4–6; 89:1; 145:4). We teach them God is mighty and tell stories of God proving Himself mighty for us. "We will not hide them from their children, but tell to the coming generation the glorious deeds of the LORD, and his might, and the wonders that he has done" (Ps. 78:4).

This extends beyond parenting to discipleship of any sort. Disciples teach and model what it means to follow Jesus, including thanksgiving. When someone gives thanks, the I-spy-God story reinvigorates everyone. Like we might do when we see an amazing sunset or a crazy deal at the store, we tell others to come see what God has done.[8]

> I have told the glad news of deliverance
> > in the great congregation;
> behold, I have not restrained my lips,
> > as you know, O LORD.
> I have not hidden your deliverance within my heart;
> > I have spoken of your faithfulness and your salvation;
> I have not concealed your steadfast love and your
> > faithfulness from the great congregation. (Ps. 40:9–10)

Notice that last line. Because of his thanksgiving stories, David claims he has not concealed God's love and faithfulness from God's people. When we keep God's praise to ourselves, we hurt the body of Christ. We have fresh food to nourish Christ's people, but rather than opening the cupboards of gratitude, we keep them shut through silence. Don't hoard God's glory.

This public praise also helps unbelievers see God. This isn't the only way we evangelize, but it substantiates and personalizes the truth from God's Word. Throughout the Gospels, Jesus' fame spreads through such stories (see Mark 7:36–37; Luke 24:48–49; John 4:28–29). People hear Jesus teach or experience His redemption and miracles. They then go tell others about it (see Luke 8:38–39). The New Testament calls Jesus' first followers "witnesses" for a reason (Acts 1:21–22). They retold what they saw and experienced.

In the Old Testament, God's people declared God's superiority over other "gods" by giving thanks before the nations (see Pss. 96:1–4; 105:1–5; Isa. 42:12; 48:20). "Declare his glory among the nations, his marvelous works among all the peoples! For great is the LORD, and greatly to be praised, and he is to be feared above all gods" (1 Chron. 16:24–25). Peter encourages believers to proclaim "the excellencies of him who called you out of darkness into his marvelous light" (1 Peter 2:9). Even if we don't sense any special blessing in our life right now, we should never get over rejoicing in God for His grace in saving us from our sin.

Through giving thanks, we point believers' eyes toward God. We disciple and pass on our faith to children and adults. And it's a nonthreatening way to brag on God and show what He's like to those who don't know Him. Make His goodness known by talking about it.

THE FINAL TOUCH

If we recognize a blessing but don't tell God thanks, our thanksgiving comes up short. It starts on the right track but stops before it reaches its destination. But as we move from feeling thankful to expressing it, the attention given magnifies our joy in the gift and Giver. It's like the final touch, sealing the deal, "Yes, I really am thankful."

Maybe this is the first time you've seen these verses. When I studied them, it surprised me how small steps of giving thanks could accomplish so much. It lit a fire of gratitude in my heart. It's not just for my good; it's for the good of others. It's an easy but significant way to point people to God. But all these benefits require the step of expressing thanks. Pastor Mark Vroegop says it this way: "When you see grace, say thanks."[9]

Putting It into Practice

SAY IT

"Let the redeemed of the LORD say so" (Ps. 107:2). Start by thinking of one thing you're thankful to God for today and then try to tell at least one person.

While this book reflects the biblical emphasis on thanksgiving being directed to God, we can foster a habit of thanksgiving by telling people thank you. As we thank them, this develops eyes to recognize reasons to give thanks and a heart willing to do so. Like Paul, we can affirm others by thanking God for His work in them by telling them what we see (Col. 1:3–8). Thank someone around you this week.

SING IT

Singing helps us vocalize truth in a way that resonates with our emotions and affections. Lyrics sung dig down and bury themselves in our brains. I still have old hymns I sang as a kid, like "It Is Well," rush to mind. This also works against us since we can't pick and choose what we remember, so unwanted songs like "Macarena" (it was the '90s) also surface.

Throughout Scripture, God's people give thanks through singing.[10] Anyone can sing and give thanks. That doesn't mean we all sound the same. I have a terrible voice. As a teenager, I once was on stage at a youth-group event to lead motions during a song. One of the singers had the bright idea of moving a microphone in front of me mid-chorus. They might have heard a "joyful noise" but it wasn't a pretty one. The face of the singer indicated that wasn't their best decision, so they quickly pulled the mic away. That was my one shot at singing with a mic and captive audience, and I don't think I'll get it back.

But God delights in our singing, not because of the quality of our voices, but because of the worship in our hearts. David penned these words: "I will praise the name of God with a song; I will magnify him with thanksgiving. This will please the LORD more than an ox or a bull with horns and hoofs" (Ps. 69:30–31). Singing gives us a chance through music and words to express our gratitude (see Pss. 30:4; 95:1–2; 147:7).

PRAY IT

Another great way to tell God thanks is spoken or written prayer. Start a habit of beginning each prayer by telling God thanks for one attribute or action of His. Read through a thanksgiving psalm or prayer and pray it back to God in your own words. Tweak your pre-meal prayer by thanking God for specific things, including but not limited to what's on your plate.

WRITE IT

Through writing, we express what we think or feel. Record specific reasons to thank God. Return to your list and recall God's work. This is one aim behind the Gratitude Challenge in the appendix. If you haven't started it or have gotten behind, start it up again.

CHAPTER 7

ENJOY THE GIFT AND EMBRACE THE GIVER

W e've looked at three features of biblical thanksgiving so far: something we're thankful for, someone we're thankful to, and expressing thanks. In this chapter, we'll unpack a fourth and final step. Giving thanks *to* God leads to joy *in* God.

When meaningful reflection rather than mindless ritual describes our thanksgiving, we know God in deeper ways. My hope is this book helps grumblers become grateful, but also that it grows our walk with Christ.

As we recognize reasons to thank someone, we discover more about them. We trace the thumbprints on the gift back to the Giver. When we do this with God's work or blessings, we not only see the good things He's done for us, but we see Him better. Joy in the Giver accompanies delight in the gift. Trillia Newbell writes, "Our enjoyment is all about him. He gives good gifts, and we in turn thank him. But we not only thank God—we experience the fullness of enjoyment as we let those gifts point us to truths about him."[1] The gift adds to our understanding of the Giver and, therefore, our joy in the Giver.

THANKSGIVING BUILDS FRIENDSHIP

Through saying thanks, we take a step closer to someone who first took a step toward us through their kind gift. Giving thanks isn't a rote act. If we mindlessly scribble words on a thank-you card and send it without a second thought, we've missed the point. But if we reflect on what their gift tells us about them, as we express our gratitude through the note, our appreciation for them increases. Thoughtfulness increases thankfulness.

As I type this, a friend is coming over to babysit our daughter. Most dinners these days stress us out. Our main aim when eating in public with a toddler is survival. If we can minimize the spills and sideway glances from others, it's a win. Only when we pay the check does the parent-sweat give way to a deep sigh of relief. We made it. Needless to say, my wife and I look forward to a relaxed dinner together.

We feel grateful for our friend making this possible. But it goes deeper when we appreciate something specific about her. We're not only thankful for babysitting, but we're thankful for her thoughtfulness in offering it. It reveals her kindness and selflessness in sacrificing a free evening for us. She could have done something else. She gave us a gift, but the gift points to her generous, considerate, and sacrificial heart. We appreciate her even more, not just for the act, but for what it shows and confirms about her. Our relationship strengthens, even if only in small degrees. But here's the kicker. If we thanked her for baby-sitting and didn't consider what it tells us about her, we might have felt grateful for the gift but it would not have deepened the friendship.

Gifts and gratitude prove most meaningful in the context of relationships. A thoughtful blessing from one person to another, and a heartfelt thanks for *both* the gift *and* the giver, bring friends closer.

In the Bible, giving thanks takes us beyond *recognizing* God and into *enjoying* Him. As we give thanks to God, we not only confess we would have nothing good apart from Him (James 1:17; 1 Cor. 4:7), but we consider who He is. Giving thanks is a relational, intimate practice stirring up love toward God. We worship God and express our joy in Him because of who He is and what He's done. John Piper says it this way:

> When the gospel of Jesus Christ frees us to see and savor the glory of God above all things, the way is opened for us to experience seamless joy in God and his gifts. We are able to see every gift as a beam from the sun of God's glory. Every joy in the beam runs up to the fountain of light and ends there. No created thing becomes a rival but only a revelation of God.[2]

Thanksgiving is a response to more than God's blessings. It's a response to what we learn about Him through them. It's more than naming or listing gifts. We also get to know the Giver.

WHY THIS MATTERS

If we miss this aspect of thanksgiving, we'll settle for a gift-focused or self-centered gratitude. The attention never shifts to God. Our trust in Him isn't stoked and the struggles of our heart aren't combated through knowing a mighty and merciful God. Gift-centered gratitude won't produce the worship, joy, and love for God that biblical thanksgiving blossoms into. But as we grow in God-centered thanksgiving, we get to enjoy the gifts and the Giver.

Understanding thanksgiving in this way, we uncover a power behind it we've missed. I'm not proposing it has a mystical, magical power released when done right, but that it's bigger and better than we realize. By giving thanks, we press into our walk with Him. We cultivate the virtue of gratitude and deepen our knowledge of God.

A BIBLICAL EXAMPLE: PSALM 107

Grab a Bible and read Psalm 107.

This corporate psalm calls on God's people to give thanks. What's the reason? God rescued them out of the painful pit of exile (see 107:3). The song mentions four groups of exiles in trials. Each is announced with the phrase "some" (107:4, 10, 17, 23), followed by a description of their circumstances. Each "cried to the LORD in their trouble, and he delivered them from their distress" (107:6, 13, 19, 28). They give thanks for their deliverance (107:8, 15, 21, 31). But they also rejoice in what each of the four mini-histories reveals about God.

The Hungry

God guides the hungry through the wilderness (107:4–9). He leads them to rest and refreshment. Through trying circumstances, their stomachs growl and hearts grumble. And then, they experience God's provision. The lesson is bigger than food. They learn through God quenching their appetite that He alone can satisfy their hungry souls. God fills their life with good things (107:9). They experience God's never-ending faithfulness.

The Powerless

As a kid, I remember watching pro wrestling on TV when Hulk Hogan was a big deal. Besides the body slam and leg drop, his patented move was ripping his shirt from top to bottom. This act proving his brute strength intimidated any opponent. It also wowed and excited his fans, the Hulkamaniacs. Kids like me watched from their living room, trying to pull apart their own shirt in like manner, only to realize they're no Hulk.

Throughout the Bible, God flexes His muscles and shows off His might by defeating the biggest and scariest enemies. Similar to how Hogan's shirt-ripping antic rallied his fans, God's powerful deeds instill confidence in His people.

Darkness engulfed the second group (107:10–16). They faced their limits and felt their powerlessness. Their dismal fate seemed just as sealed as their prison cell. No doubt you've been in a spiritual dungeon like this before. You might have heard the heavy clink of the dead bolt on the other side of the door. Both light and hope were shut out. But then like Hulk Hogan emerging from backstage and running into the ring, God enters the story and everything changes. He saves the day. He exercises His jaw-dropping strength by delivering His people. The most daunting opponent stands no chance against the almighty God.

Powerless people aided by a powerful God can overpower any obstacle.

He sets the prisoners free, kicking down the doors of jail cells and breaking iron bars like they're nothing (107:14, 16). Though God's people are weak, their God isn't. He delivers them from distress and death (107:13–14). The strength of God flashes before them. Thankfulness for rescue points them to a God who will not leave or forsake them. They grasp God's strength on display through the gift of deliverance and freedom. They're grateful for such a gift, and awed by the God who supplied it.

The Broken

God also heals and restores the foolish who brought pain into their lives (107:17–22). Like I leave my dresser drawer open at night, only to slam into it in the dark, Judah's foolishness brought affliction into their path. Though their ways led to destruction (107:17–19), God saves them. He makes whole the broken. God heals our wounds, whether self-inflicted or from another. They offer sacrifices of thanksgiving (107:22), not only for the gifts received but as a way to rejoice in the God of grace. God's not only mighty; He's merciful. They give thanks to God for restoring them, but even more so, they can be grateful for a God full of patience, forgiveness, and grace. Their gratitude to God grows their love for God.

The Fearful

The fourth group faces a terrifying storm (107:23–32). Though threatening waves towered above them, God proved creation is no match for its Creator. Winds and waves obey Him. That's true with a storm in nature or a trial in life. He can calm the waters and silence the strongest squall.

But He might not. He might use the storm for a season to strengthen our faith. There's no promise when or if it will cease in this life, but there is a promise that God will carry us through it.

In this case, the God who stirred up the storm (107:25) now stills it (107:29). He quiets the weather and quiets their hearts. He brings them safely to their destination (107:30). They see the wondrous works of the Lord (107:24) and praise Him (107:32). God spares their life, but He also proves His power and authority. They gain firsthand knowledge of God's sovereign rule over the weather, His good purposes for them, and His commitment to carry them safely through whatever they face.

Each of these wondrous works prove the goodness and steadfast love of God (107:1, 8, 15, 21, 31). They give thanks for what God's done for them *and* for what it says about Him. Both the gift and the revelation of God through it bring joy. Thanksgiving joins gift and Giver. They now not only have a temporary blessing, they gain greater knowledge of and love for their covenant-keeping God.

Thanksgiving is a conduit of communion with God. God's attributes and actions open windows to see who He is. Through giving thanks to God, we get more of God in return. These small investments of thanksgiving pay huge dividends.

HOW TO DO THIS

Let me provide a few examples of how reflecting on God's gifts increases thankfulness for and knowledge of the Giver. We can give thanks in big and small things, trials and blessings.

Car Repairs

When things break in my car or in my house, it stresses me out. I'm not a handyman. I can fill up my car tires and paint walls, but my skills stop there. There's the work of figuring out who to call, scheduling an appointment, and determining if I trust what they tell me needs to be done. Do I need a new furnace or not? Is that rattling in the car normal? I don't know, and they're the expert, so there goes my money.

He's likely rounding the rough edges off my entitled, whining heart that feels like nothing should break and everything should be easy.

Even in these things, I can give thanks. I thank God for providing financially so I can get problems fixed. I thank Him for the people who do the repairs and the skills they possess. This small annoyance forces me to trust God knows I needed this in my life right now. Maybe He wants to teach me patience or dependence on Him, or help me not take blessings for granted. Maybe God wants to show His faithfulness despite the financial setback. He's likely rounding the rough edges off my entitled, whining heart that feels like nothing should break and everything should be easy.

This tells me God wants me to be Christlike more than He wants my comfort. I can thank God for the inconvenience because His purposes are good. Not all gratitude is easy. As I choke out grumbling by giving thanks in the repair shop's lobby, my heart leans into what I know to be true about God, and what this small test might further reveal. It's a gift because God is good and at work, even if I don't like the packaging it comes in. But if I never pause to trust and thank God, I'll miss what He's doing.

Maple Syrup

Thank God for condiments. To be honest, maple syrup is more than a condiment in my house. We like pancakes, waffles, and French toast, but those are sponges soaking up the star of the show: maple syrup. It even elevates bland breakfast items like granola or oatmeal into an edible treat.

Growing up, my parents put the cheap "imitation syrup" on my plate. Only as an adult were my eyes opened with the discovery of 100% pure maple syrup (the darker the better). Every time I eat maple syrup—or taste test a spoonful to make sure it's still good (don't judge me)—I thank God for filling the earth with little pleasures. God could have created the world and cut out the extra gifts like this, but He didn't. Maple syrup reveals a God who not only provides, but gives pleasure. He's generous and goes above and beyond meeting our needs. Just like I enjoy blessing my child with small gifts because her happiness gives me joy, God delights in giving us good things and seeing us relish them.

Friends

Though God's review of everything else in creation was "good," He said it was "not good" for man to be alone (Gen. 2:18). No one is an island. We need others, and not just dogs or cats, Siri or Alexa, or even books. We're created for relationships.

Paul's letters are full of thanksgiving for friends and ministry partners. God works in our life through people, such as when Paul is comforted by Titus (2 Cor. 7:6). Paul's greetings usually move from thinking of them to thanking God for them (Eph. 1:15-16; Phil. 1:3; Col. 1:3).

When God puts family or friends in your life, thank Him. Seasons where relationships seem scarce teach us how valuable friendships are. When I give thanks to God for life-giving relationships, I thank Him for putting people in my life who help me flourish. He's a kind Father who knows we won't do well in isolation. God cares for us and matures us by providing friends and fellowship. He's looking out for us in these gifts.

God's Word

Bibles are commonplace in America. I can buy one at a dozen local stores. Between my house and office, I couldn't tell you how many I own. And yet, having a Bible in my language is a priceless treasure.

Every time you open God's Word, thank Him for it. Through Scripture, God reveals what's true, good, and beautiful. We know God's purposes and will for us because of it. Authors recorded in it the good news of salvation in Christ alone by grace alone through faith alone.

As we give thanks for the Bible, we thank God for the incalculable gift of revealing Himself to us. God could have kept a distance from us, but He makes Himself known. As Francis Schaeffer noted, He is there and He is not silent. I thank the God who overflows with love for us and to us. I thank Him that (and this truly is stunning) He genuinely wants me to know Him and be in a warm, close relationship with Him.

God's Righteousness

God's actions and attributes call for worship-saturated thanksgiving. You could pick any attribute of God and meditate on it, thanking Him for all it shows us about what God is like.

Consider God's righteousness. There is no evil, wickedness, or impurity in God. None. God is perfect. He's just, upright, holy, and faithful in all He does. Old Westerns (which I'm a fan of) show the value of a person whose word is their bond. God never goes back on His word or compromises His integrity. He is true and trustworthy.

The Bible talks about God's righteousness enduring forever or stretching to the heavens like a mountain (Pss. 36:6; 111:3).

I thank God that His perfect righteousness doesn't come or go depending on His mood; it's constant and unchanging.

My sinful, prideful heart is too quick to question Him. As I give thanks to God for His righteousness, it reassures me everything He does is right. It convinces me to plead my case with Him or bring injustices in the world to Him. The more I thank God for His righteousness, the more I'm awed by His glory and see Him as a rock I can depend on. I know I can take His Word and promises to the bank. He always comes through.

Reflecting on these gifts leads to rejoicing in the Giver. In biblical thanksgiving, rather than good things competing with God, they help us know Him.

STUDY THE WORKS OF GOD

The Bible calls us to not only recognize God's works (a first step) but to study them. "Great are the works of the LORD, studied by all who delight in them" (Ps. 111:2). Through this study and reflection on God's person, acts, and gifts, we better grasp His goodness, grace, and glory. David meditated on all God has done (Ps. 143:5). When we go beyond what we're thankful for, and consider what it tells us about God, it endears us to Him.

Romans 1 concludes the same thing from the opposite angle. The ungrateful fail to discern what God reveals in creation (Rom. 1:21). Rather than seeing God's "eternal power and divine nature" (1:20) and giving thanks, they suppress these truths through ingratitude. We either study God's works with thanksgiving, or suppress them in ingratitude. Gratitude draws us near to God. Ingratitude pushes Him away.

Thanksgiving, at its best, involves saying thanks to God for His works *and* worshiping God because of what those things tell us about Him. What He does helps us know who He is. Giving thanks starts with something but expands to Someone.

Through this study and reflection on God's person, acts, and gifts, we better grasp His goodness, grace, and glory.

I hope this doesn't sound daunting. It will stretch us, and like anything new, it might be difficult at first. Start by giving thanks to God. As you do that, take a few seconds to linger. Whatever attribute, blessing, work, or activity of God you're giving thanks for, ask what it shows you about Him. What does it reveal about who He is? What truths about God does it highlight or reinforce?

In my own journey of replacing grumbling with gratitude, learning to see and know God more through thanksgiving deepened my appreciation for it. I learned the only way to "do all things without grumbling" (Phil. 2:14) was to instead give thanks in all things. Every day, every circumstance, every opportunity provided me a chance to express gratitude and eradicate grumbling. Though it started with recognizing God's gifts and saying thanks, over time I grew in understanding who God is and how He's at work through those gifts. My view of God increased and my trust in God strengthened. As I taught others about how to enjoy the Giver through thanksgiving for what He gives, I saw the same joy and growth in their lives. Thanksgiving proved to be not only biblical but beneficial. It's powerful because it lifts our eyes upward to our glorious and gracious God. I pray that as you practice thanksgiving, you would experience the power of seeing, knowing, and enjoying God in a similar way.

Gratitude is an act of obedience, but it's also an act of worship that motivates obedience. As giving thanks helps us better see who God is, it leads to knowing, loving, and trusting Him. We grow through gratitude.

Putting It into Practice

GRATITUDE CHALLENGE

As you participate in the Gratitude Challenge, you'll record daily things you're thankful for. As you do this, reflect on what these blessings reveal about God.

PSALM 145

Psalm 145 is a thanksgiving psalm. Study it as a springboard to give thanks. You can read it and pray back short prayers of thanksgiving, or try the exercise outlined below.

1. Circle any words related to ways we give thanks: extol, bless, praise, thank, commend, declare, meditate, speak, sing, tell . . .

2. Underline any reasons for which David gives thanks. For example, because "Great is the LORD," He is "to be praised" (145:3). In this sentence, circle "praised" and underline "Great is the LORD."

3. Review the underlined reasons David thanks God. Which highlight an attribute of God and which mention an action, work, or gift of God? (There will be overlap, so choose the one you think is primary.) Put a "1" next to those pointing out an attribute of God and a "2" by God's actions.

4. Do any of those phrases resonate with something God has done in your life? To use 145:8 as an example, God is gracious and merciful to us in many ways, but does a specific instance come to mind (such as the way He restored you after you fell into sin)?

5. Work through the psalm, giving thanks to God. You could divide it into three sections of seven verses.

CHAPTER 8

REMEMBERING: LOOKING BACK TO LOOK FORWARD

My wife and I love to travel. We enjoy day trips around Indiana, extended weekends, trips to see family in nearby states, and vacations to new destinations. We like the shared experiences inherent in travel: the memories made (some joyful and some stressful), the food and drink tasted, sights seen, beauty taken in, pictures snapped, and learning what makes a place unique.

I'm the nostalgic one. I overspend on souvenirs, postcards, and knickknacks as part of treasuring our trips. At each destination, we buy a Christmas ornament and a travel mug. I consider coffee one of those new morning mercies God daily gives (Lam. 3:23). Each morning we drink fresh coffee from one of these mugs. It's a way to reminisce about the places we've been.

When guests visit our home and we serve them a cup of quality coffee (a gift all good hosts should offer), they often ask about the mug they're drinking from. This gives us a chance to share our experiences, retell stories, and recount favorite memories tied to those locations.

Remembering in this way, even with a small, insignificant coffee mug, brings the past into the present. In the Bible, God commands storing up memories—in recorded stories, memorials and monuments, food and drink, and through festivals and special days—to teach us about who He is. The walk down memory lane gives ample opportunities to sing God's praise and give thanks. Grateful remembering compels us to turn and trust today in the one who proved Himself trustworthy in the past.

DILIGENT MEMORY

Remembering spiritual truths seems like it should be easy. It's not. We quickly forget God or drift toward spiritual amnesia. We dismiss what God has done for us or taught us. Trying circumstances and bitter temptations appear rosier in the rearview mirror.

God knows our weaknesses, including our forgetfulness. But He also recognizes how much remembering bolsters our faith. He instructs us to remember and warns against forgetting. Tony Reinke writes, "*Remembering* is a key verb of the Christian life. We recall our past, we correct our nearsightedness, we take heart, we regain mental strength, we find peace in the eternal Word. Remembering is one of the key spiritual disciplines we must guard with vigilance amid the mind-fragmenting and past-forgetting temptations of the digital age."[1]

In this chapter, I want to show how the Bible links thanksgiving and remembrance to strengthen God's people when they're weak. Christians must draw from the well of their memories and histories to find refreshment in God's faithfulness.

Charles Spurgeon called this "diligent memory." "Memory seems to lie in two things: first, in retaining an impression, and then in recollecting it at a future time."[2] Reflecting on God's works invites us to give Him thanks. Thanks to God produces trust in God. Trust helps us see God's glory. The bigger God becomes in our mind's eye the smaller our problems become. Not because they aren't real or scary, but because they shrink in a side-by-side comparison to God.

Throughout Scripture, God's people remember His works, promises, and character. It's not a way to swap stories and re-member the good ole times. We *must* remember because we need to look back to find grounds to trust in God. Present fears and future anxieties are calmed by past faithfulness—not our faithfulness but God's faithfulness. Remembering generates thanksgiving.

> **Christians must draw from the well of their memories and histories to find refreshment in God's faithfulness. . . . Present fears and future anxieties are calmed by past faithfulness—not our faithfulness but God's faithfulness. Remembering generates thanksgiving.**

WHAT KIND OF REMEMBERING?

The wise words of a grandparent, falling in love, the trials of teen-age years, conversion, a bad decision or regretful moment, the kind act of someone, a book, a song, or precious moments from your child's life—these can all be memories that move us. As the gears of our memories wind up, they turn the wheels of our perceptions, thoughts, moods, desires, and will. This can guide us forward into light and wisdom or, when they bring up guilt or hurt, they can take us down a dark and destructive path. Memories lead us closer to God or further from Him.

By remembering, we tell ourselves what is true and what happened in the past so we can massage the truth into our heart. Theologian Michael Horton explains this biblical conception of affective remembering:

> In our Western (Greek) intellectual heritage, "remembering" means "recollecting": recalling to mind something that is no longer a present reality. Nothing could be further from a Jewish conception. For example, in the Jewish Passover liturgy, "remembering" means participating here and now in certain defining events in the past and also in the future.[3]

Paul uses memory to motivate gospel unity through diversity: "Remember that you were at that time separated from Christ, alienated from the commonwealth of Israel and strangers to the covenants of promise, having no hope and without God in the world. But now in Christ Jesus you who once were far off have been brought near by the blood of Christ" (Eph. 2:12–13).

Moses warned God's people about the danger of forgetting: "Only take care, and keep your soul diligently, lest you forget the things that your eyes have seen, and lest they depart from your heart all the days of your life" (Deut. 4:9).

Remembering is an action-oriented word. By calling something to mind, it changes us.

I'm only in my first decade of marriage, but I know the importance of remembering our wedding anniversary. *How* I remember makes all the difference. If I did nothing out of the ordinary, failed to give her a gift, or ignored any additional words of kindness, it wouldn't go well. If I said to her: "Today is our anniversary. I'm noting it and remembering it," but I did nothing loving for her that day, I've blown it. She wouldn't say, "How thoughtful! I'm glad you didn't forget." Having it on my calendar and making a mental note isn't remembering.

You don't remember by stating the facts: "Our wedding was one year ago." My wife would expect remembering our anniversary to stir different actions from the day before, such as me writing her a warm note or taking her on a date. And not just any date, like another trip to Chick-fil-A, but a splurge kind of date. We remember our covenantal promise as I pursue, cherish, and love her afresh as I vowed on our wedding day.

Remembering stirs our affections, but not just with sentiment and nostalgia. It recalibrates us around some key truth, lesson, conversation, or reality worthy of holding on to. Memories influence us as long as they stay with us. Not only because our past is an essential part of who we are, but because in reaching back into the saved files of our mind we can be taught, consoled, or motivated. They are not distant occurrences but living impressions.

DAVID'S EXAMPLE

After a gauntlet of genealogies (chapters 1–9), David takes center stage in the historical record of 1 Chronicles. He prioritizes worshiping God in his political agenda. Though he expands Israel's rule, suffers attacks from inside and outside, falls into personal sin, experiences betrayal, and endures family calamities, David seals his legacy by his pursuit of God.

The special presence of God required David's retrieval of the ark of the covenant (but not like Indiana Jones in *Raiders of the Lost Ark*). The ark represented God's power and presence. Its return to Jerusalem and a specially prepared tent (1 Chron. 16:1) calls for celebration. With the ark's return, David renews sacrificial worship, blesses the people, and bestows on them gifts of food: bread, meat, and cakes. (Call it the "David diet" and put me on it.) He appoints priests to lead God's people by invoking, thanking, and praising the Lord (16:4). On the first day, David assigns Asaph to lead a song of thanksgiving.* Before reading through this song, I want to put three things on your radar. I list them in advance so you can better spot them.

First, notice the part thanksgiving plays in worshiping God. It's not merely one aspect of worship, but giving thanks *is* what they do when they worship. All worship is grounded in gratitude.

---

* While Asaph likely sang the entirety of Psalm 105 at this event, the author of Chronicles leaves out the Exodus portion (Ps. 105:23–45) and focuses on God's promise keeping to Abraham and the patriarchs. Both texts draw on history to stir gratitude toward God.

Look for the role of remembering. This song retells a part of Israel's story. It looks back with eyes open to God's covenant faithfulness to a wandering people. In both hills and valleys, God led His people, and the songwriter thanks Him for His wondrous works.

Third, don't miss how the backward-looking song awakens future-oriented prayer (16:35–36). Though Israel celebrates today, they do so aware of the troubles and challenges on the horizon. Connect the dots as you trace the path from remembering to thanking to trusting.

> Oh give thanks to the LORD; call upon his name;
>> make known his deeds among the peoples!
> Sing to him, sing praises to him;
>> tell of all his wondrous works!
> Glory in his holy name;
>> let the hearts of those who seek the LORD rejoice!
> Seek the LORD and his strength;
>> seek his presence continually!
> Remember the wondrous works that he has done,
>> his miracles and the judgments he uttered,
> O offspring of Israel his servant,
>> children of Jacob, his chosen ones!
>
> He is the LORD our God;
>> his judgments are in all the earth.
> Remember his covenant forever,
>> the word that he commanded, for a thousand
>>> generations,

the covenant that he made with Abraham,
>   his sworn promise to Isaac,
which he confirmed to Jacob as a statute,
>   to Israel as an everlasting covenant,
saying, "To you I will give the land of Canaan,
>   as your portion for an inheritance."

When you were few in number,
>   of little account, and sojourners in it,
wandering from nation to nation,
>   from one kingdom to another people,
he allowed no one to oppress them;
>   he rebuked kings on their account. . . .

Oh give thanks to the LORD, for he is good;
>   for his steadfast love endures forever!

Say also:

"Save us, O God of our salvation,
>   and gather and deliver us from among the nations,
that we may give thanks to your holy name
>   and glory in your praise.
Blessed be the LORD, the God of Israel,
>   from everlasting to everlasting!"

Then all the people said, "Amen!" and praised the LORD.
(16:8–21, 34–36)

This testimony of God's supremacy shows up in His covenant-keeping with Israel. Asaph moves from the patriarchs

(16:16–22; Ps. 105:9–15) to deliverance from Egypt (Ps. 105:23–42) to entrance into Canaan (Ps. 105:43–45). The turns and twists might look different, but God remains the same.

God is faithful, even when we're unfaithful. God kept His promise made to Abraham, Isaac, and Jacob by bringing Israel into Canaan (1 Chron. 16:16–18). His Word never fails. Never. Though Israel was few in number, lacked power, and remained helpless on their own, God protected them. He delivered them from all their enemies (16:19–21). He shows steadfast love and unending mercy despite their wayward hearts.

Each trying circumstance opens a door for hope as God bursts onto the scene to prove His name and promises. Despite your wandering heart, God holds and keeps you. He brought you through the years and sustained you along the way. It might have required Him to pick you up and carry you in His strong arms through some deep waters or dark tunnels, but you're here. Your history proclaims the kindness, power, and grace of God. Whether reading Scripture or recalling your story, there's no shortage of opportunities to remember with thanks.

Asaph, and Israel collectively, takes this opportunity with the ark's arrival to be wowed by the ways of God. He doesn't settle for pointing God's people to general ideas or spiritual platitudes about God. He gets specific and personal by drumming up the works of God on their behalf.

Every memory of God's acts sheds light on His character. This remembering is a means of giving thanks and it multiplies into giving thanks. The more they remember the more they rejoice. Charles Spurgeon adds, "Lay up this great goodness in your memory to be the material for future psalms of praise. . . . Let every personal mercy be written upon your personal memory."[4] Remembering is the music sheet teaching us how to sing God's praises through every line and stanza of our memories.

Notice how praising God bleeds into petitioning God.[5] "Oh give thanks to the LORD, for he is good; for his steadfast love endures forever! Say also: *'Save us,* O God of our salvation, and *gather and deliver us* from among the nations, that we may give thanks to your holy name and glory in your praise'" (16:34–35, emphasis added). Though thanksgiving might be the theme of the song, it's not where the song ends.

Saying "thank you" often leads to the requests of "please" or "more." John Piper explains, "Gratitude exults in the past benefits of God and says to faith, 'Embrace more of these benefits for the future, so that my happy work of looking back on God's deliverance may continue and increase.'"[6] Thankful praise motivates trustful prayer.[7] God's people ask for the kind of things they've seen Him do historically. The God who delivered Israel from other nations in the past (16:19–22) can deliver them from nations in the present (16:35). The God of salvation who redeemed Israel from bondage to Egypt (Ps. 105:26–38) can save them now (1 Chron. 16:35). They don't panic because of what they're up against. They bring the past to bear on the present and fear gives way to faith.

In other words, the psalmist says to God, "I know You can deliver us now because You've delivered us so many times before. We thank You for what You've done and for what You will do." Their personal history overflows with examples of God's faithfulness and power.

The same process of looking back in grateful remembrance

to find faith for looking ahead applies to us. Remembering allows us to proclaim: God is mighty, and I can thank Him right now because these are the ways He's been mighty in my life. God is kind and gentle because in these specific times He acted kind to me. I know God is merciful and gracious because in my sin, God poured out grace.

Praises for God's faithfulness in our past lead to prayers for continued faithfulness today and tomorrow.

REMEMBER. THANK. TRUST.

My wife and I recently took time to answer the question, "What can we thank God for from the past year?" There are lots of ways to answer that question, including the countless blessings stacking up day after day. For us it was a chance to look back with our heads above water. A year prior, our family was walking through one of those dark, foggy valleys. With the arrival of our first child—a daughter we love and thank God for daily—we faced many unexpected challenges.

A baby surfaces hidden idols for parents who built too much of life around themselves (getting to do what they want when they want and how they want it). The change isn't difficult for some, but it was a painful process for us. We struggled with the lack of sleep, decreased income, health scares, missing social events for early bedtimes, comparing our child to others, and the isolation of parenting.

It's not only true that every couple experiences parenthood differently, but so does each spouse. The life transitions hit my wife harder than me. During this stretch of time there were many days she felt discouraged, overwhelmed, anxious, empty, and unsure how she would make it in this new role. Though not always in the same darkness myself, as the spouse of someone walking through this, it weighs on you. Some days I was empathetic and tried to carry burdens with her. On other days, I fought frustration, wanting her to move past it all. There were many days of praying, and some days you struggle to pray because you wonder why God hasn't made it easier.

Like most trials, it lasted longer than we would have liked. There were days life pressed out of us all emotional and spiritual strength. But like all desert seasons I've walked through, eventually God led us out of the valley and we again felt the warm rays of sunshine against our faces. Not all struggles were erased, but He brought us through and we sensed the worst of the storm had passed.

Sitting on our couch answering what we were thankful for from the past year provided a moment to recount this history together. We saw His kindness, faithfulness, care, and provision in countless ways. His goodness was evident in removing idols from the clutches of our hands. By faith we believed He would use us to comfort others with the same comfort we received (2 Cor. 1:3–7). In many of our anxieties and discouragements, God lovingly provided some unexpected blessing to boost our spirits and give hope. Through it all, God was good.

In recounting the ups and downs of the past year, we found many reasons to thank God. We didn't have all the "why" answers for what we walked through but we did clearly see God's hand. He proved in our lives what the Word tells us about His grace being sufficient and His promises to uphold us. As remembering led to thanksgiving, it gave strength and hope to trust Him with whatever's next.

Even now when feeling overwhelmed or discouraged, I look back with thanks as a means of looking forward with trust. Some days I pray, "God, You have been (fill in the blank: good, kind, faithful, merciful, powerful) in the past, so I trust You will be so again now." Or "God, You have done (fill in the blank), so I know You can do it again. Help me now."

Recalling God *was* good reassures us God *is* good now and God *will be* good tomorrow. A track record of trust leads to thankfulness, but it also boosts our faith, so we say, "Do it again."

Look back in grateful remembrance so you can look forward in confident hope. When has God proven Himself in the past? How has God flexed His muscles to give power when you needed it? In what ways has God been gracious and good to you?

Shift your posture and eyes upward to God. You have a list (conscious or not) of challenging circumstances and stresses on your plate. But do you have your list of God's faithfulness and former deeds? What can you thank God for from today, this week, or this year? Write these things down. Store up memories of God's works so you have reasons to give thanks, but also so you have reason to trust. It's hard for distress or anger—or whatever your struggle is—to find room in a heart full of praise.

Don't view thanksgiving as something to tack on when things are good or in one month of the year. It's the means by which we plant our feet in the firm footing of God's steadfast love in the past so we have traction to walk forward. God remains full of steadfast love, unlimited power, unending wisdom, and inexhaustible grace. You don't have to push through with gritted teeth, carrying these burdens on your own scrawny spiritual shoulders. Look back and give thanks. Trust God. Believe in Him to do today what He did in the past.

Putting It into Practice

GIVE THANKS TOGETHER

Giving thanks isn't a solo task. You should give thanks to God on your own, but we also should do it with others. Ask at a meal, "What's one thing God has done or taught you recently that you're thankful for?" Use holidays to reflect on God's goodness and faithfulness in recent months. Use gatherings with believers—formal or informal—to cultivate a practice of remembering and thanksgiving. Encourage others with something you've recently seen in God's Word. Ask people to share stories of God's work or promises fulfilled. Follow up on prayer requests as a way to look back and to thank God. Be the kind of person who ignites sparks of gratitude wherever you go and in all your relationships.

Some days you'll be able to offer this and some days you'll be empty and desperately need it yourself. Invite others to speak truth into your life with encouragement of God's faithfulness, His promises, and the gospel. Because we forget, we need faith-forming friendships pointing one another back to Him.

THE LOCAL CHURCH

There are many ways your local church can promote these disciplines. Encourage people to share testimonies or life stories—not only of salvation but of God's ongoing work—in as many settings as possible: Sunday morning, prayer services, ministries, small groups, and Bible studies.[8]

Whether it's through a mural or through a story written somewhere visible, tell the church's story. As a church, remember God's mercy and power in starting and sustaining your church. Lift up baptism and communion as the signs and symbols given to the church to remember. If you're an elder, pastor, or staff member, build this rhythm of remembrance into meetings. Encourage people with a more seasoned faith to disciple those younger in the faith, including sharing stories of what God taught them over the years. Send your pastors or elders encouraging emails about what God has done for you or why you're thankful to Him. Give a grateful testimony in your small group or Bible study.

Remember. Give thanks. Trust. Look forward in faith by looking back in thanks.

CHAPTER 9

GRITTY GRATITUDE: GIVING THANKS IN ALL CIRCUMSTANCES

Last weekend, my wife, daughter, and I were in Michigan visiting family. As we dressed for church on Sunday morning, my wife put my daughter's hair in a ponytail and felt something on her neck. It was a tick. Gross, I know. The kids played outside the day before and it must have hitched a ride and camped out for the night.

Everyone had left the house, and we were alone. Like good millennials with our first child, we panicked. Not on the outside, since kids are like bears in that they sense fear. But inside, the alarms blasted and whistles blew. We not only hear news reports about the rising prevalence of tick-borne Lyme disease, but we have several families in our church suffering through it.

Our limited knowledge told us not to burn it out (which people apparently try), since putting a flame to our daughter's

THE GRUMBLER'S GUIDE TO GIVING THANKS

skin seemed like a bad idea. We also knew if we pulled it out ourselves but did it wrong, it might go in deeper or get stuck. We ended up taking her to urgent care—in a town we had no idea where to go.

Since all of this happened as I'm writing this book, I tried to practice what I write. Though worry had the upper hand in my heart, I wanted to fight back by turning to God in thanksgiving. But in the moment, what do you give thanks for? Do I thank God for allowing her to get a tick that might give her a disease? (That didn't seem right.) Do I thank Him for us finding the tick?

I'll come back to this question, but let me share how the rest of the morning went. We drove to the closest urgent care. Because we arrived before their normal opening time, we waited in the parking lot for fifteen minutes. When it rains it pours, so the office was closed that day.

My two-year-old handled things pretty well. To prepare her, I told her she had a bug in her neck and would need to see the doctor so he could help. She seemed to find this amusing. During the car ride, she repeatedly told us she had a bug in her neck. She's two, and television makes all critters seem lovable, so in her mind a tick is the same as a friendly little caterpillar.

The story ended well. We sped to the next urgent care a couple miles away. The doctor removed the still-living tick. We watched it crawl around the medicine bottle the doc placed it in. He informed us the tick wasn't engorged and must not have been there long. He also told us the tick wasn't the kind that carried Lyme. Deep exhale.

I'll admit, it was easier to give thanks on the way home than it was on the earlier drive. We could now thank God the doctor removed it. We helped Lily tell God thanks for urgent care offices, nurses and doctors, and for medicine (antibiotic cream in this case). Lily enjoyed telling everyone about her experience of having a bug in her neck, visiting the doctor, and seeing the tick once they quarantined it in a bottle. I don't know what happens to these ticks, but I assume it's a fitting end and they don't live happily ever after.

Let's go back to my earlier question: What do you give thanks for in the heat of the moment? What could I have thanked God for in the car on the way to the urgent care? Did I need to give thanks at all? Are some moments for giving thanks and others exempt? It even raised theological questions. If I can thank God for His hand in helping us locate the tick early, why couldn't He have kept her from getting one in the first place?

We'll come back to this scenario at the end of the chapter. As we consider why we can give thanks in all circumstances, it might provide insight into my situation. I picked an example from everyday life, knowing there are bigger challenges, trials, and pain we'll walk through than the example above. But whether it's a frustrating inconvenience or a life-altering tragedy, how do we give thanks in all circumstances?

This chapter won't answer every question about suffering, but I hope it can teach us how and why to give thanks when life is hard. We can give thanks, not because we always feel grateful or like what's happening, but because we trust God. Melissa Kruger writes, "The bedrock of our rejoicing isn't the goodness of our day but the goodness of our God."[1] We rest in His goodness, love, and sovereignty, and we say thanks for what He's doing in all things.

Thanksgiving is a trusting response that proclaims God is good and so are *all* His ways. Even in hard things, God is faithful. He's with us and at work for us.

FAITH OVER FEELINGS

In this book, we've talked a lot about giving thanks for blessings, though I've tried to include thanksgiving for God's plan, purposes, and attributes. We give thanks *in all circumstances* because thanksgiving extends beyond blessings. We love God's works and Word, not just His wallet. We desire God's presence in addition to His provision. And we need the glory of who God is even more than we need good things He gives.

We give thanks when we feel grateful, but we also give thanks when we don't. It doesn't require feelings; it requires faith. Faith trusts that God cares, He's in control, and He's working all things for my good. With thanksgiving, faith (rather than feelings) is the power source.

That's why I've emphasized the action of giving thanks more than the emotion or disposition of gratitude. Emotions aren't unimportant; they just can't be ultimate or authoritative. We *should* cultivate gratitude to God. I've given ideas for doing so throughout the book. But giving thanks doesn't require experiencing gratitude first. Even if discouraged, empty, or struggling to rest where God has us right now, we can give thanks because hope in Him outweighs our momentary experience.

I don't wait until I have a fuzzy feeling to do something loving for my wife. I wouldn't leave the dishes piling up in the sink or choose not to make my wife hot tea (usually requested right after I sit down) because I don't *feel* a strong impulse of love at that moment. I do love her, and this is bigger than emotions (though it should include them); it doesn't require me to feel something to do what I know is right.

The same is true for giving thanks. Pursue things that stir up gratitude. But don't wait for a mood of gratitude to strike you before giving thanks. More often than not, the action helps quicken the emotion. As we practice thanksgiving, we experience gratitude where it had been missing.

ALL CIRCUMSTANCES? REALLY?

A few key Pauline texts call us to give thanks in all circumstances. Let me remind you, he wrote some of these words in prison. Paul doesn't prod us toward thanksgiving from an ivory tower. He pens them as a captive facing impending death. But nothing, not prison, pain, or even death, will silence his praise.

> Giving thanks always and for everything to God the Father in the name of our Lord Jesus Christ. (Eph. 5:20; see also Col. 3:17)

> Rejoice always, pray without ceasing, give thanks in all circumstances; for this is the will of God in Christ Jesus for you. (1 Thess. 5:16–18)

> Rejoice in the Lord always; again I will say, rejoice. Let
> your reasonableness be known to everyone. The Lord
> is at hand; do not be anxious about anything, but in
> everything by prayer and supplication with thanksgiving
> let your requests be made known to God. And the peace
> of God, which surpasses all understanding, will guard
> your hearts and your minds in Christ Jesus. (Phil. 4:4–7)

Most agree Paul isn't suggesting we thank God for every single thing. How can we give thanks for things God opposes? The wise words of R. C. Sproul explain Ephesians 5:20.

> Oftentimes these words are misappropriated to say more
> than the text actually says. "For everything" must be
> interpreted consistent with the last clause, "in the name
> of our Lord Jesus Christ." If the meaning of the term "for
> everything" is devoid of reference to God's character,
> purpose and nature, grave distortions can occur. Some,
> in "literal" zeal, actually thank God for things he de-
> spises. This faulty thinking drives some to the conclusion
> they must thank God for the very evil he hates.
>
> May this never be. We dare not thank God for evil
> consequences of sinful actions, such as when a drunken
> driver kills another person. What we praise God for is
> for being God in the midst of such terrible tragedies, and
> for his redeeming purposes which can bring light out of
> darkness. There is a multitude of things to thank God for
> in the midst of tragedies, but these must be consistent
> with his character and redeeming purposes. Exhaust

those things in prayer, and do not be tempted to offer indiscriminate praise to the offence of God.[2]

In everything, even in the worst of things, God has not stepped down from His throne or abandoned His good purposes. God has not left us or forsaken us. As hard or frustrating as circumstances might be, God will use it for good. That's a fact. The Bible doesn't say God *might* or *could* use hard things for the good of His people; it says He *will* do this (Rom. 8:28; Eccl. 8:12).

Israel might not have given thanks for wilderness experiences like deadly serpents, starvation, and delayed answers to God's promises, but they could give thanks God was at work through these things (Deut. 8:7, 15). He carried them safely through it. He provided. He sustained. He worked in mighty ways. For all these things, they gave thanks. This doesn't eliminate their cries, tears, or the blisters on their feet. It doesn't wipe away the stinging memories of lost loved ones or the unfulfilled longings of their heart for home. And yet, through the whole wilderness trial, God led them through these things "to do [them] good in the end" (Deut. 8:16). For that, they gave thanks.

God's people turn to thanksgiving in trying circumstances (Pss. 9; 31; 118; Phil. 4:4–9; Luke 22:14–23). Even in the potholes of life, our situation might be tough, but it's never void of reasons for gratitude.

> **Even in the potholes of life, our situation might be tough, but it's never void of reasons for gratitude.**

DAVID'S EXAMPLE

Groaning and gratitude can coexist. We don't have to choose between tears and thanks. In hard things, we can ask God for help and tell Him thanks. We can lament what's broken or painful while giving thanks for good things, even if that's God's presence, provision, or plan. Since thanksgiving is God-centered rather than gift-centered, we can give thanks in all seasons and circumstances.

It's easy to practice gleeful gratitude in blessing, but mature faith needs just as much a gritty gratitude in difficulties.

David models this trust in God producing thanks to God. The church needs more of this. We're quick to complain and quit. We get knocked off our horse and lie there for a while rather than jumping back on. Our faith needs true grit that endures and presses on. It's easy to practice gleeful gratitude in blessing, but mature faith needs just as much a gritty gratitude in difficulties. We discover this not by looking inside or sucking it up through willpower; we find it by turning to God.

Psalm 28

I know it's easy to distance ourselves from Moses or Mary, David or Deborah. Not only did they live in a far-off place, but they're in the Bible. We forget these are real people, and the Bible exposes them as frail sinners like you and me. These are no Goody Two-shoes who don't struggle with fear, doubt, and depression. They weren't immune to sin. They didn't live out their lives knowing they'd be Bible characters one day.

When we read about David's enemies surrounding and threatening him, he likely felt fear similar to what we experience (see Ps. 56:3). The "what if" questions must have run through his mind. What will happen to my family and nation? Will we survive? The self-doubt crept in. Will we win? Will everyone turn on me? David knew difficult days. And David learned how to respond with trust-oriented thanks.

In Psalm 28, David cries out for mercy and protection. He needs God's strong defense department against his enemies, and God's grace for the fear and dread overwhelming him. And so he gives thanks. "Blessed be the LORD! For he has heard the voice of my pleas for mercy. The LORD is my strength and my shield; in him my heart trusts, and I am helped; my heart exults, and with my song I give thanks to him. The LORD is the strength of his people; he is the saving refuge of his anointed" (Ps. 28:6–8). Expressing gratitude stirs up and seals in him the faith and strength he needed.

It would have been easy for David to grumble, and it would have been natural to feel justified in his worry, but he redirects both his tongue and his heart through giving thanks. He fights powerful temptation, pushes back on his crushing worries, and leans into the unshakable faithfulness of God through thanksgiving. It doesn't change his circumstances, but it does change his perspective.

Psalm 35

David can in one breath lament life's difficulties and in the next breath give thanks. In Psalm 35, he laments[3] how God's enemies seem to get away with evil while he agonizes through suffering and being maligned.

> Malicious witnesses rise up;
>> they ask me of things that I do not know.
> They repay me evil for good;
>> my soul is bereft.
> But I, when they were sick—
>> I wore sackcloth;
>> I afflicted myself with fasting;
> I prayed with head bowed on my chest.
>> I went about as though I grieved for my friend or my
>>> brother;
> as one who laments his mother,
>> I bowed down in mourning.

> But at my stumbling they rejoiced and gathered;
>> they gathered together against me;
> wretches whom I did not know
>> tore at me without ceasing;
> like profane mockers at a feast,
>> they gnash at me with their teeth.

> How long, O Lord, will you look on?
>> Rescue me from their destruction,
>> my precious life from the lions! (Ps. 35:11–17)

Teetering on the edge of despair, the throbbing of a crushed heart breathes out the "How long, O Lord?" question. What counsel do you give a friend leveled by suffering? What encouraging word do you speak? What thought might lift them off the floor? When you find yourself there, where do you go?

Even as David utters his cry for help, notice the words that follow. "I will thank you in the great congregation; in the mighty throng I will praise you" (35:18; see also Ps. 22:22–26). A discouraged, wounded heart can find healing in lament and hope in thanksgiving. Both shift our eyes away from the circumstances and onto God.

I'm not saying we can't voice our raw emotions and pains to God through lament or that we have to maintain an optimistic "when life gives you lemons, make lemonade" attitude. But David demonstrates in his laments that even when things are hard, there's room to give thanks. Christians can be "sorrowful, yet always rejoicing" (2 Cor. 6:10). God is big enough to carry us through our pain or trial. We give thanks because we know the current difficulties will not last forever. God will never abandon us. He always hears our cries. And we thank Him for what we know to be true even while we lament what feels so painful.

A discouraged, wounded heart can find healing in lament and hope in thanksgiving. Both shift our eyes away from the circumstances and onto God.

Charles Spurgeon offers a model from church history of choosing gratitude over grumbling. Spurgeon endured frequent assaults from the enemy. In addition to all the normal struggles of life, he suffered from gout and other health conditions that often kept him from the pulpit for extended seasons. Fellow pastors and local newspapers alike criticized him and slandered his name. He persevered through bouts of depression, experienced tragedies such as when a panic during his preaching led to seven people being trampled to death, absorbed the blows from controversies and division from other churches, and labored under the ceaseless demands of the ministries he oversaw. And yet, when you read the sermons and books of Spurgeon, he was a man acquainted with both grief and gratitude. He wrote, "Remember the mercies of God. Do not bury them in the grave of ingratitude. Let them glisten in the light of gratitude."[4] Because we put our hope and trust in God, we can be people grieving pain and still give praise.

FOUR WAYS TO RESPOND IN TRIALS

Here are four ways to choose giving thanks. Think of these as a map for gritty gratitude, charting a way forward when we feel lost or discouraged.

1. Rest in God's Sovereign Plan

The basis of giving thanks isn't gifts; it's God. It's not *liking* everything God gives us but *trusting* He knows best. God blesses us with many gifts. But God also allows trials and suffering for our good (1 Peter 1:6–9; 2 Cor. 4:17; Phil. 3:10).

Truth anchors us in storms. You might not give thanks for the specific details of a trial, but you can thank God for who He is in it. God is not only the ultimate object of our thanksgiving; He's the ultimate source. We "rejoice always" because we rest in

God's sovereign plan. No matter what, God is in control. God cares. He's at work to do you good. He's with you.

Rest in the one who reigns.

2. Cling to God's Good Promises

God's promises are gifts. Even when we can't spot blessings around us, we turn to His promises. In most trials, there are many unknowns. There's a lot of uncertainty and not a lot to hold on to. But we can cling to God's promises. Thanksgiving depends on God's character, not His blessings. Because God is unchanging, His promises are firm. Because God is good, so are all His promises.

Suffering is not the final word in our suffering—hope is. Charles Spurgeon wrote, "For humanity, amid all its sorrows and sins, hope sings on. . . . Because our hope abides, our praise continues."[5] *Hope sings on.* We find our voice for giving thanks in hope through God's promises. Where our feet feel like slipping, these provide traction for us to take steps forward.

When nothing is stable, cling to God through His precious promises.

3. Look for God's Evident Work

While we can give thanks even when we can't yet see the sun through the fog, it does help when we find small reasons to give thanks. Start with low-hanging fruit. Look for where God's work is clear. Spot blessings, however small or few, and say thanks. This shifts our mindset away from grumbling and toward gratitude.

The famous hymn "Count Your Blessings" offers this counsel:

> When upon life's billows you are tempest-tossed,
> When you are discouraged, thinking all is lost,
> Count your many blessings, name them one by one,
> And it will surprise you what the Lord has done.[6]

Financial counselor Dave Ramsey talks about the "snow-ball effect" when paying off debt. He recommends paying off the smallest debts first. As you cross them off the list, you gain energy that helps you tackle the bigger, scarier hurdles. The same snowball effect applies to gratitude. As we give thanks for blessings, it builds momentum. Gratitude grows. We perceive reasons to give thanks we might otherwise miss. During a trial, look for God's work and give thanks where you can. As your heart feels tiny ripples of gratitude, ride them as the waves get bigger and bigger.

4. Trust in God's Steadfast Love and Faithfulness (Even When You Don't See It or Feel It)

There will be times where we don't see the good in a situation. After most of the wilderness seasons I've endured, I can look back and see what God has done through them. But that doesn't mean everything will be like this. Some things won't make sense to us this side of heaven.

Giving thanks depends on trusting God to do good, not in seeing the good. This isn't blind faith but trust built on God's faithfulness. We trust in a good, loving, all-knowing, sovereign God. Sometimes a posture of thankfulness means saying, "God,

I can't see what You're doing, and this feels hard. But I trust You. And I want to trust You. Help me. You are good, in control, with me, and at work. Thank You."

BACK TO THE TICK

Returning to my story about the nasty tick: How should I have prayed on the way to the urgent care facility? As fear and worry spread, what could I give thanks for? Here's how I could practice thanksgiving in those moments based on the four ways to respond we've look at.

I thanked God this was not taking Him by surprise. He knew this would happen. He wasn't fearful or stressed like we were. God remained sovereign. My trial didn't derail His plan. I could thank Him that He was in control, which meant I didn't have to be.

The next thing I turned my attention to were God's promises. These provide a steady floor when our world feels wobbly. God promises to work all things for our good. God promises to be with us, even through fires and storms. He never promised we wouldn't experience difficulties or would be immune to pain, but He promised to sustain us and walk with us. Knowing these promises of God gave me specific things I could give thanks for.

Even though my mind gravitated to worries and fears, it helped to look for reasons to give thanks. I could thank God we found the tick when we did. I thanked Him for having a place to take her, medical professionals who could help, and an open facility on the weekend.

Finally, we entrusted her to God. I not only had to do this in the car that day, but as a parent, every day I face something that worries me. In these moments, I pray back a promise made in her child dedication by surrendering all earthly claims and control over her. God is in control; I'm not. She's in God's hands; not mine. And He's trustworthy and faithful.

GIVE THANKS

Maybe suffering or sorrow weighs you down today. It might tempt you to believe thanksgiving isn't for you. But we know that can't be the case because God tells us we can give thanks in all circumstances. Both the happy and the heartbroken can give thanks because God is constant in all circumstances. He is present and powerfully at work, whether seen or unseen. Turn to Him. Thank Him. Trust Him.

Putting It into Practice

THE GOOD, THE BAD, AND THE UGLY

Think about one trial, challenge, or struggle in life right now. Work through the four steps outlined in this chapter. How can you rest in God's control? What promises can you cling to? What can you thank God for, even in hard things? Why can you trust God, no matter what?

Write down the circumstance troubling your heart. Then list three to five things you can thank God for in this. Maybe it's something God is doing through it. It could be a blessing in disguise, or a promise of God you're holding on to. Maybe it's an attribute of God you're leaning into. But through ugly, broken scenarios, what can you still give thanks for?

As you face trials and frustrations, you can either grumble against God or give thanks to God. Grumbling pushes us away from Him, but thanksgiving draws us near to Him. Remember that giving thanks is for all circumstances, not just the good times. That doesn't mean we deny hardship or must "think happy thoughts" all the time. Spiritual maturity doesn't require fleeing to a spiritual Neverland where nothing goes wrong, the burdens of life are ignored, and life is a dream come true. We can and should lament, as we saw from David's example in Psalm 35, but we can simultaneously give thanks. We can be honest with God in lament about why something is hard, while entrusting what's hard to Him and thanking Him for the good things we trust He is doing. Joy and sorrow aren't mutually exclusive, and neither are lament and thanksgiving. Learn to live with both as regular rhythms in your walk with Christ.

As you continue to grow in gratitude, do so by cultivating a gut response of giving thanks to God. Because God is good *all the time*, we never run out of reasons for thanksgiving. Grumblers don't become grateful by avoiding or outlasting problems.

Grumblers become grateful by trusting God through practicing thanksgiving, even when it's hard.

READ THE PSALMS

The Psalms express all the emotions we feel, and they speak into a breadth of life experiences. They teach us how to give thanks in every season and circumstance. Read through the Psalms and look for the themes related to thanksgiving. Learn from this wonderful book of the Bible when to give thanks and how to do so.

GRATITUDE CHALLENGE

The goal of this Thirty-Day Challenge is to cultivate the rhythm of giving thanks. We don't change through good intentions unless they're met by moving in a new direction. That takes time and consistency. Drew Dyck explains: "Forming a new habit (especially a good habit) is a tremendous draw on your willpower reserves. Initially the new behavior may be physically or mentally challenging. It will cut against the grain of your natural inclinations. It takes effort. Lots of it."[1]

Unlike vowing off sugar forever, or your New Year's resolution to work out every day for an hour, growing in gratitude is a realistic resolution. But let grace motivate you, not guilt. If you forget or fail one day, start fresh the next day. Find a friend or two to take this challenge with you to provide mutual encouragement and accountability.

We'll learn about the Bible's emphasis of giving thanks through reading each day and practice it by recording what we can thank God for and telling Him thanks. Our objective is to be thankful for God's gifts and grow in loving and knowing Him as the Giver.

While this Challenge is flexible as to how and when you use it, consider using it during a season like Lent, Advent, or in the month of November. Or ask your Bible study, small group, friends, or family to do it with you for one month.

The Challenge consists of three elements.

1. **Read and meditate on the Bible verses about giving thanks**. See below for a thirty-day list.

2. As you read God's Word about gratitude, **include a prayer of thanksgiving.** Thank God for what you've learned about who He is, what He's done, or the gifts He's given.

3. During the day, **look for things God is doing for which you can give thanks**. Keep a journal, a scrap paper on your desk, or use a notes app on your phone, but find a way to record things you're thankful for. Set a goal of writing down five things each day.
   This doesn't always have to be spiritual. One day you might thank God for the forgiveness given through Christ, and the next day you might thank God for good football. Not all gifts are equally valuable but all gifts can be a source of thanksgiving.

Join others taking the Gratitude Challenge by using social media to show something you're thankful to God for. Use the hashtag #gratitudechallenge when you post it.

THIRTY-DAY READING PLAN

Below are thirty passages on various aspects of thanksgiving. As you read them, notice how God is thanked, what He's thanked for, and the results of giving thanks. Let it lead you into seeing God at work in your own life and thanking Him for it. Reflect on what they teach you about thanksgiving or reasons to give thanks. Then give thanks to Him in prayer.

1. Matthew 7:9-11; James 1:17; 1 Corinthians 4:17; Romans 11:36
2. Daniel 2:17–23; 6:10; Romans 8:28–29
3. Psalm 100
4. Luke 17:11–19
5. 1 Chronicles 29:10–22; Leviticus 7:11–15
6. Romans 1:18–23; 12:1–2
7. Psalm 103
8. John 6:11, 23; 11:41; Acts 27:33–38; 1 Timothy 4:3–4
9. Philippians 4:4–9; 1 Thessalonians 5:16–18; 1 Peter 5:6–9
10. Exodus 14:10–14; 15:22–16:8; Philippians 2:14
11. 1 Chronicles 16:1–36
12. Psalm 9
13. Psalm 28
14. Psalm 136
15. Romans 6
16. Psalm 33

17. Matthew 26:26–29; Hebrews 8:6–13
18. Psalm 30
19. 1 Timothy 1:12–17; Ephesians 2:1–10; 2 Corinthians 4:15
20. Psalm 95
21. Psalm 118
22. 1 Samuel 8
23. Deuteronomy 8
24. Ephesians 1:3–14
25. 1 Corinthians 15:12–28, 35–58
26. Psalm 105
27. Psalm 104
28. Psalm 138
29. Psalm 145
30. Revelation 4:1–11; 7:9–17

ACKNOWLEDGMENTS

Publishing a book is never one person's project. It requires the contribution of many, from those who encouraged the author to keep going to editors knee-deep in details. I've been supported, encouraged, and helped by fellow church members and pastors, my family, friends, and the Moody Publishers team.

I'm grateful to Moody Publishers for giving me the opportunity to write this book. It's a joy and honor to write for Moody. The Moody Bible Institute was formative in my ministry training and personal growth. Thank you to Amy Simpson for your guidance on this work from proposal to publication, and Connor Sterchi for your editing services.

For me, writing is a community project, birthed out of ministry and friendships in the church. Thank you to the elders, staff, and members at Pennington Park Church (formerly College Park Church Fishers) and College Park Church for giving me a place to encourage the body of Christ through teaching and writing. Thank you to those who read portions of the book's manuscript and offered insightful feedback: Andy Cassler, Katie Elliott, Leanne Fuhs, Brad Merchant, and Mark Vroegop.

I'm grateful to Hannah Anderson for adding her words to this book through the foreword. Your books, articles, and tweets (or threads) have been an encouragement to me, as was your writing advice about pointing out and adding to the goodness in the world.

And I especially want to thank my wife and daughter. Of all the good earthly gifts God's given me, you two are the best. Thank you, Melissa, for your partnership in life, prayers in this process, and your selflessness in allowing me to spend late nights and early mornings writing. And to you, Lily, thank you for being my little adventurer, eager to see and delight in the good gifts God scattered throughout His world.

For all these gifts, I give thanks to the God who gives them.

NOTES

Introduction: Confessions of a Recovering Pessimist

1. Ann Voskamp's *One Thousand Gifts* taught me to observe rather than overlook blessings. David Pao's *Thanksgiving: An Investigation of a Pauline Theme* provided a biblical, God-centered foundation.

Chapter 1: Gratitude's Blueprint

1. Cornelius Plantinga Jr., *Assurances of the Heart: Faith-Building Devotions on Questions Christians Ask* (Grand Rapids: Zondervan, 1993), 62.
2. Tim Keller (@timkellernyc), Twitter, November 22, 2018, 5:23 a.m., https://twitter.com/timkellernyc/status/1065566310699024384.
3. For more on enjoying God's gifts without idolizing them, I recommend these books: Trillia Newbell, *Enjoy: Finding the Freedom to Delight Daily in God's Good Gifts* (Colorado Springs: Multnomah, 2016); Joe Rigney, *The Things of Earth: Treasuring God by Enjoying His Gifts* (Wheaton, IL: Crossway, 2014); John Piper, *God Is the Gospel: Meditations on God's Love as the Gift of Himself* (Wheaton, IL: Crossway, 2005).
4. Piper, *God Is the Gospel*, 141.
5. David Pao, *Thanksgiving: An Investigation of a Pauline Theme* (Downers Grove, IL: Apollos, 2002), 28–29.

Chapter 2: A Theology of Thanksgiving

1. We will talk about giving thanks by using these related words, including drawing from Scriptures that do the same.
2. The same is true of words like *bless*, *extol*, and *give thanks*. See Psalms 118:26, 28; 145:10.
3. While "praise" is often used in a context of singing, this is not always the case (see 1 Chron. 16:7; Pss. 28:7; 33:2). "Even if distinctions between thanksgiving and praise can be made in the Old Testament, such distinctions dissolve in the theology of Paul." David W. Pao, *Thanksgiving: An Investigation of a Pauline Theme* (Downers Grove, IL: InterVarsity Press, 2002), 27.
4. See also Neh. 12:40–43; 1 Chron. 29:6–13; 2 Chron. 29:31, 36; Pss. 9:14; 92:1–4; 107:22; 118:21–29; Phil. 1:3–4.
5. David Pao, *Thanksgiving: An Investigation of a Pauline Theme* (Downers Grove, IL: InterVarsity Press, 2002), 102.

Chapter 4: Recognize. Reflect. Receive.

1. A great help for understanding the problems busyness creates and how we might live differently is *Crazy Busy: A (Mercifully) Short Book about a (Really) Big Problem* (Wheaton, IL: Crossway, 2013) by Kevin DeYoung.
2. Adele Calhoun, *Spiritual Disciplines Handbook: Practices That Transform Us* (Downers Grove, IL: InterVarsity Press, 2015), 89.
3. Chapter 1 of Alan Noble's book *Disruptive Witness* highlights the barrier of distraction and the effects on the Christian life. Alan Noble, *Disruptive Witness: Speaking Truth in a Distracted Age* (Downers Grove, IL: InterVarsity Press, 2018). See also Tony Reinke, *12 Ways Your Phone Is Changing You* (Wheaton, IL: Crossway, 2017).
4. Jon Bloom, "Lord, Deliver Me from Distraction," Desiring God, December 6, 2016, https://www.desiringgod.org/articles/lord-deliver-me-from-distraction.
5. Tish Harrison Warren, *Liturgy of the Ordinary: Sacred Practices in Everyday Life* (Downers Grove, IL: InterVarsity Press, 2016), 135.
6. Charles Spurgeon, *The Practice of Praise* (Springdale, PA: Whitaker House, 1995), 19.
7. Another practical book on learning to observe God's gifts is *The Practice of Praise* by Charles Spurgeon.
8. Ann Voskamp, *One Thousand Gifts* (Grand Rapids: Zondervan, 2010), 54.
9. Voskamp, *Gifts*, 118.
10. Ragan Sutterfield, *Wendell Berry and the Given Life* (Cincinnati: Franciscan Media, 2017), loc. 950, Kindle. Berry's fictional story *Hannah Coulter* beautifully embodies this in one woman's story.
11. Warren, *Liturgy of the Ordinary*, 136.
12. Johnson Oatman Jr., "Count Your Blessings," 1897, accessed June 26, 2019, https://library.timelesstruths.org/music/Count_Your_Blessings/.

Chapter 5: Look Around and Look Up

1. See 1 Chron. 29:10–22; Ps. 111:2–3; Dan. 2:20–23; Matt. 7:9–11; John 3:27; 1 Cor. 15:10; 1 Tim. 4:4–5.
2. Nancy Leigh DeMoss, *Choosing Gratitude: Your Journey to Joy* (Chicago: Moody Publishers, 2009), 38. Italics original.
3. This doesn't mean all people experience common grace gifts at all times or in the same ways. A home to sleep in is a common grace blessing because it's not peculiar to believers, but some people live in homes whereas others might sleep in a hotel, stay with friends, live outdoors, sleep in a shelter, or be homeless.
4. See Pss. 19:1–6; 104; 111; 145:10; 147:7–20; Isa. 40:12, 28; Jer. 32:17; Rom. 1:18–22.
5. Charles Spurgeon, *The Practice of Praise* (Springdale, PA: Whitaker House, 1995), 18.
6. DeMoss, *Choosing Gratitude*, 35.
7. The Old Testament often connects thanksgiving to God with His "steadfast

love." See Ezra 3:11–12; 1 Chron. 16:34; Ps. 100:4–5; 106:1; 107:1, 8; 118:1, 29; 136 (repeated); 145:8–10.

Chapter 6: Thankfulness Expressed

1. C. S. Lewis, *Reflections on the Psalms* (San Diego: Harcourt, 1958), 95.
2. See 1 Chron. 16:8–9; Pss. 9:1–14; 26:7; 95:1–2; 105:1; 106:1–2; 107:2, 8, 21–22; 145:4–7, 10–12, 21; Jer. 30:19; Jonah 2:9; Eph. 5:4, 20; Col. 3:15–17; Heb. 13:15.
3. Here's a sample of verbal expressions of giving thanks in the Bible. Sing aloud (Ps. 9:1–2). Tell (26:7). Make known (105:2). Utter the mighty deeds of the Lord (106:2). Declare His praise (106:2). Proclaim aloud (26:7). Commend (145:4). Speak (145:6, 21). Pour forth His fame (145:7). Bless (145:10). Voice (Jonah 2:9). Offer up a sacrifice of praise (Heb. 13:15). Acknowledge His name (Heb. 13:15). Shout (Isa. 12:6). Make a joyful noise (Ps. 95:2). Pray (John 6:11).
4. Charles Spurgeon, *The Practice of Praise* (Springdale, PA: Whitaker House, 1995), 27.
5. Paul Tripp, @PaulTripp. October 19, 2016, 7:18 a.m. tweet.
6. Gary Thomas, *The Glorious Pursuit: Embracing the Virtues of Christ* (Colorado Springs: NavPress, 1998), 139.
7. Spurgeon, *The Practice of Praise*, 31.
8. See also 1 Chron. 16:8–9; Pss. 9:11; 89:1; 145:11–12; Col. 3:15–17; Eph. 5:20.
9. Mark Vroegop, "Goal," sermon delivered at College Park Church, December 1, 2019, https://www.yourchurch.com/sermon/goal/.
10. See also Ps. 28:7; 30:4; 69:30; 95; 100; 105:1–2; 136; 138:1–2; 147:7; 1 Chron. 16:8–36; Ezra 3:11; Col. 3:16; Isa. 12:3–5.

Chapter 7: Enjoy the Gift and Embrace the Giver

1. Trillia Newbell, *Enjoy: Finding the Freedom to Delight Daily in God's Good Gifts* (Colorado Springs: Multnomah, 2016), 4.
2. John Piper, *God Is the Gospel: Meditations on God's Love as the Gift of Himself* (Wheaton, IL: Crossway, 2005), 141.

Chapter 8: Remembering: Looking Back to Look Forward

1. Tony Reinke, *12 Ways Your Phone Is Changing You* (Wheaton, IL: Crossway, 2017), 188.
2. Charles Spurgeon, *The Practice of Praise* (Springdale, PA: Whitaker House, 1995), 20.
3. Michael Horton, *The Christian Faith: A Systematic Theology for Pilgrims on the Way* (Grand Rapids: Zondervan, 2011), 799.
4. Spurgeon, *The Practice of Praise*, 17, 23.
5. For a New Testament example, Paul's thanksgiving report in Colossians 1:3–8 flows into the prayer report of 1:9–14.
6. John Piper, *Future Grace: The Purifying Power of the Promises of God* (Colorado Springs: Multnomah, 2012), 36–37.

7. Also note the ending of verse 35 returning to thanksgiving as a yielded trust in God. Praise leads to petition, and when we petition God in prayer we wait in a posture of praise.

8. For more on the value of remembering together, see my article, "Your Church Needs More Time for Personal Testimonies," 9Marks, August 19, 2019, https://www.9marks.org/article/your-church-needs-more-time-for-personal-testimonies/.

Chapter 9: Gritty Gratitude: Giving Thanks in All Circumstances

1. Melissa B. Kruger, *In All Things: A Nine-Week Devotional Bible Study on Unshakeable Joy* (New York: Multnomah, 2018), 78.

2. R. C. Sproul, *The Purpose of God: Ephesians* (Fearn, Scotland: Christian Focus Publications, 1994), 128.

3. To better understand lament, see Mark Vroegop, *Dark Clouds, Deep Mercy: Discovering the Grace of Lament* (Wheaton, IL: Crossway, 2019).

4. Charles Spurgeon, *The Practice of Praise* (Springdale, PA: Whitaker House, 1995), 76.

5. Spurgeon, *The Practice of Praise*, 35.

6. Johnson Oatman Jr., "Count Your Blessings," 1897, accessed September 3, 2019, https://library.timelesstruths.org/music/Count_Your_Blessings/.

Gratitude Challenge

1. Drew Dyck, *Your Future Self Will Thank You: Secrets to Self-Control from the Bible and Brain Science (A Guide for Sinners, Quitters, and Procrastinators)* (Chicago: Moody Publishers, 2019), 127.

Feeling worn thin? Come find rest.

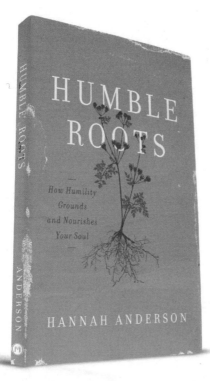

NEW RELEASES FOR CULTIVATING CHARACTER

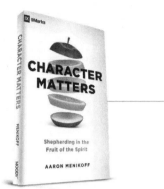

Character Matters will help ministry leaders slow down, cut through distractions, and focus on what matters—the fruit of the Spirit. As you spend time focusing on the simple things that matter, you'll see your heart and ministry, slowly but surely, changed by the power of the Spirit.

978-0-8024-1974-3

On Waiting Well identifies the experience of waiting as a crucial dimension to loving God, having faith, and following Christ. Discover how waiting is integral to God's plans of life and salvation. When we gain that perspective, these seemingly dry times become invigorating opportunities to strengthen our hope in God who is always faithful.

978-0-8024-1967-5

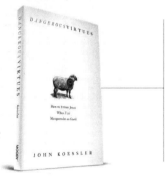

When sin is disguised as virtue, the path to cultivating righteousness becomes impossible. *Dangerous Virtues* examines how to recognize these seven deadly sins as they are subtly disguised in today's culture. Christians must develop a discerning eye in a world where good is called evil and evil called good.

978-0-8024-1964-4

Also available as eBooks

MOODY
Publishers®

From the Word to Life®

What if your ordinary interactions with family, neighbors, and coworkers are actually invitations to adventure with God?

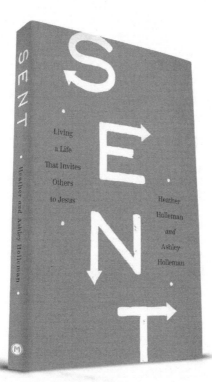

GET THE RESOURCES YOU NEED FOR WHEN LIFE TAKES AN UNEXPECTED TURN.

978-0-8024-2332-0   978-0-8024-2338-2   978-0-8024-2341-2   978-0-8024-2343-6

978-0-8024-2344-3   978-0-8024-2345-0   978-0-8024-2359-7   978-0-8024-2360-3

Be it in the midst of a natural disaster, global unrest, or an unforeseen pandemic, the repercussions of unprecedented change can leave us all reeling. Get the wisdom, encouragement, and peace you need to ease your anxieties, strengthen your relationships, and encounter the almighty God during such trying times.

also available as eBooks

MOODY
Publishers®

From the Word to Life®